Obsessive-Compulsive

About the authors

Jonathan S. Abramowitz, PhD, is Professor and Associate Chair of Psychology and Research Professor of Psychiatry at the University of North Carolina (UNC) at Chapel Hill. He is Director of the UNC Anxiety and Stress Disorders Clinic and a North Carolina licensed psychologist with a diplomate from the American Board of Professional Psychology. He is an international expert on anxiety and OCD and has published 12 books and over 200 research articles and book chapters. He is editor of two scientific journals, including the *Journal of Obsessive-Compulsive and Related Disorders*. Dr. Abramowitz has served as President of the Association for Behavioral and Cognitive Therapies.

Ryan Jane Jacoby, MA, is a doctoral student of clinical psychology in the Anxiety/OCD Lab at the University of North Carolina (UNC) at Chapel Hill. She conducts research on the nature and treatment of OCD and anxiety disorders, and is specifically interested in cognitive biases, treatment augmentation strategies, symptom dimensions of OCD, and inhibitory learning approaches to exposure therapy. Ms. Jacoby has published and presented her research at various national and international professional conferences and has received numerous awards for her academic accomplishments.

Advances in Psychotherapy – Evidence-Based Practice

Series Editor
Danny Wedding, PhD, MPH, School of Medicine, American University of Antigua, St. Georges, Antigua

Associate Editors
Larry Beutler, PhD, Professor, Palo Alto University / Pacific Graduate School of Psychology, Palo Alto, CA
Kenneth E. Freedland, PhD, Professor of Psychiatry and Psychology, Washington University School of Medicine, St. Louis, MO
Linda C. Sobell, PhD, ABPP, Professor, Center for Psychological Studies, Nova Southeastern University, Ft. Lauderdale, FL
David A. Wolfe, PhD, RBC Chair in Children's Mental Health, Centre for Addiction and Mental Health, University of Toronto, ON

The basic objective of this series is to provide therapists with practical, evidence-based treatment guidance for the most common disorders seen in clinical practice – and to do so in a "reader-friendly" manner. Each book in the series is both a compact "how-to" reference on a particular disorder for use by professional clinicians in their daily work, as well as an ideal educational resource for students and for practice-oriented continuing education.

The most important feature of the books is that they are practical and easy to use: All are structured similarly and all provide a compact and easy-to-follow guide to all aspects that are relevant in real-life practice. Tables, boxed clinical "pearls," marginal notes, and summary boxes assist orientation, while checklists provide tools for use in daily practice

Obsessive-Compulsive Disorder in Adults

Jonathan S. Abramowitz

Ryan J. Jacoby

University of North Carolina at Chapel Hill

Library of Congress Cataloging in Publication
information on the print edition is available via the Library of Congress Marc Database under the
Library of Congress Control Number 2014953725

Library and Archives Canada Cataloguing in Publication
Abramowitz, Jonathan S., author
    Obsessive-compulsive disorder in adults / Jonathan
S. Abramowitz, Ryan J. Jacoby (University of North Carolina
at Chapel Hill).

(Advances in psychotherapy--evidence-based practice ; v. 31)
Includes bibliographical references.
Issued in print and electronic formats.
ISBN 978-0-88937-411-9 (pbk.).--ISBN 978-1-61676-411-1
(pdf).--ISBN 978-1-61334-411-8 (html)

    1. Obsessive-compulsive disorder--Treatment. 2. Evidence-
based psychiatry. I. Jacoby, Ryan J., 1987-, author II. Title.
III. Series: Advances in psychotherapy--evidence-based practice
v. ; 31

RC533.A29 2014   616.85'227   C2014-907056-X
                                            C2014-907057-8

© 2015 by Hogrefe Publishing
http://www.hogrefe.com

PUBLISHING OFFICES
USA: Hogrefe Publishing Corporation, 38 Chauncy Street, Suite 1002, Boston, MA 02111
              Phone (866) 823-4726, Fax (617) 354-6875; E-mail customerservice@hogrefe.com
EUROPE: Hogrefe Publishing GmbH, Merkelstr. 3, 37085 Göttingen, Germany
              Phone +49 551 99950-0, Fax +49 551 99950-111; E-mail publishing@hogrefe.com

SALES & DISTRIBUTION
USA: Hogrefe Publishing, Customer Services Department,
              30 Amberwood Parkway, Ashland, OH 44805
              Phone (800) 228-3749, Fax (419) 281-6883; E-mail customerservice@hogrefe.com
UK: Hogrefe Publishing, c/o Marston Book Services Ltd., 160 Eastern Ave.,
              Milton Park, Abingdon, OX14 4SB, UK
              Phone +44 1235 465577, Fax +44 1235 465556; E-mail direct.orders@marston.co.uk
EUROPE: Hogrefe Publishing, Merkelstr. 3, 37085 Göttingen, Germany
              Phone +49 551 99950-0, Fax +49 551 99950-111; E-mail publishing@hogrefe.com

OTHER OFFICES
CANADA: Hogrefe Publishing, 660 Eglinton Ave. East, Suite 119-514, Toronto, Ontario, M4G 2K2
SWITZERLAND: Hogrefe Publishing, Länggass-Strasse 76, CH-3000 Bern 9

Hogrefe Publishing
Incorporated and registered in the Commonwealth of Massachusetts, USA, and in Göttingen, Lower Saxony,
Germany

Printed and bound in the USA

ISBN 978-0-88937-411-9 (print) • ISBN 978-1-61676-411-1 (PDF) • ISBN 978-1-61334-411-8 (EPUB)
http://doi.org/10.1027/00411-000

Preface

This book describes the conceptualization, assessment, and psychological treatment of obsessive-compulsive disorder (OCD) in adults using empirically supported cognitive-behavioral (CBT) interventions. The centerpiece of this approach is *exposure and response prevention* (ERP), a well-studied tandem of techniques derived from learning theory accounts of OCD. Recent scientific and clinical advances, however, have led to fine-tuning ERP in ways that can improve its delivery to maximize adherence and outcome. Most notably, the fields of cognitive therapy, acceptance and commitment therapy (ACT), couple therapy, and inhibitory learning have implications for ERP for OCD that we have incorporated into this book. We assume the reader – psychologists, psychiatrists, social workers, students and trainees, and other mental health care practitioners – will have basic knowledge and training in the delivery of psychotherapeutic intervention, yet not necessarily be a specialist in OCD. This book is for clinicians wishing to learn therapeutic strategies for managing OCD effectively in day-to-day clinical practice.

The book is divided into five chapters. The first describes the clinical phenomenon of OCD, differentiating it from other problems with similar characteristics and outlining scientifically based diagnostic and assessment procedures. Chapter 2 reviews leading theoretical approaches to the development and maintenance of OCD, and their treatment implications. In Chapter 3, we present a framework for conducting an initial assessment and for deciding whether a particular patient is a candidate for the treatment program (as discussed in Chapter 4). Methods for explaining the diagnosis of OCD and introducing the treatment program are incorporated. Chapter 4 presents in detailed fashion the nuts and bolts of how to conduct effective CBT for OCD. There are numerous case examples and transcripts of in-session dialogues to illustrate the treatment procedures. The chapter also reviews the scientific evidence for the efficacy of this program and discusses how to identify and surmount a number of common obstacles to successful outcomes. Finally, Chapter 5 includes a series of case examples describing the treatment of various sorts of OCD symptoms (contamination, fears of responsibility for harm, etc.). A variety of forms and patient handouts for use in treatment appear in the book's appendix.

OCD is a highly heterogeneous problem. Some patients experience fears of germs and contamination, while others have recurring unwanted anxiety-evoking ideas of committing heinous acts that they are unlikely to commit (e.g., deliberately running into pedestrians while driving). It is rare to see two individuals with completely overlapping symptoms. Thus, we provide a multicomponent approach that guides the clinician in structuring treatment to meet individual patients' needs. In this book you will find practical clinical information and illustrations along with supporting didactic materials for both you and your patients.

Acknowledgments

We are indebted to a large group of people, including series editor Danny Wedding and Robert Dimbleby of Hogrefe Publishing for their invaluable guidance and suggestions. The pages of this book echo with the clinical wisdom we have acquired through direct and indirect learning from masters of the science and art of psychological theory and intervention, including Joanna Arch, Donald Baucom, David A. Clark, Michelle Craske, Edna Foa, Martin Franklin, Michael Kozak, Jack Rachman, Paul Salkovskis, and Michael Twohig.

We dedicate this book to our patients and research participants who come to our clinic seeking help and, in the face of uncertainty, find the courage to confront their anxieties and give up their compulsive behaviors so that they can achieve a better quality of life. They believe in us, confide in us, challenge us, and educate us.

Dedication

To our parents, Ferne and Leslie Abramowitz; Doug and Jennie Jacoby

Table of Contents

1

Description

1.1   Terminology

Obsessive-compulsive disorder (OCD) (300.3) was previously classified as an anxiety disorder in DSM-IV. In DSM-5 (American Psychiatric Association, 2013), it is the flagship diagnosis of the obsessive-compulsive and related disorders (OCRDs), a category of conditions with putatively overlapping features (see Section 1.5).

1.2   Definition

OCD is defined in the DSM-5 by the presence of *obsessions* or *compulsions* (see Table 1). Obsessions are persistent intrusive thoughts, ideas, images, impulses, or doubts that are experienced as unacceptable, senseless, or bizarre and that evoke subjective distress in the form of anxiety or doubt. Although highly specific to the individual, obsessions typically concern the following themes: aggression and violence, responsibility for causing harm (e.g., by mistakes), contamination, sex, religion, the need for exactness or completeness, and serious illnesses (e.g., cancer). Most patients with OCD experience multiple types of obsessions. Examples of common and uncommon obsessions appear in Table 2.

Definition of obsessions and compulsions

Compulsions are urges to perform behavioral or mental rituals to reduce the anxiety or the perceived probability of harm associated with an obsession. Compulsive rituals are deliberate, yet excessive in relation to, and not realistically connected with, the obsessional fear they are performed to neutralize. As with obsessions, rituals are highly individualized. Examples of behavioral (overt) rituals include repetitious hand washing, checking (e.g., locks, the stove), counting, and repeating routine actions (e.g., going through doorways). Examples of mental rituals include excessive prayer and repeating special phrases or numbers to oneself to neutralize obsessional fear. Table 3 presents examples of some common and uncommon compulsive rituals.

Table 1
DSM-5 Symptoms of OCD

Time-consuming (e.g., 1 hr or more) obsessions or compulsions that cause marked distress and impairment in social, occupational, or other areas of functioning

Obsessions:
Repetitive and persistent thoughts, images, or impulses that: (a) are experienced as intrusive and unwanted, (b) cause anxiety or distress, and (c) are not worries about real-life problems. The person tries to ignore or suppress the thoughts, images, or impulses, or neutralize them with some other thought or action.

Compulsions:
Repetitive behaviors or mental acts that are performed in response to an obsession or according to certain rules. Compulsions are aimed at preventing or reducing distress or preventing feared consequences; yet are clearly excessive or are not linked in a realistic way with the obsession.

Insight: The person might have varying levels of insight into the validity of her or his obsessions and compulsions, ranging from good or fair insight, to poor insight, to no insight. The level of insight might change with time and vary depending on the particular theme of obsessional fears.

Tics: Some people with OCD have tic-like OCD symptoms that are characterized by a distressing sensory (somatic) state such as physical discomfort (e.g., in the neck) which is relieved by motor responses that resemble tics (e.g., stretching, eye blinking).

Table 2
Common and Uncommon Obsessions

Common obsessions
- The idea that one is contaminated from dirt, germs, animals, body fluids, bodily waste, or household chemicals
- Doubts that one is (or may become) responsible for harm, bad luck, or other misfortunes such as fires, burglaries, awful mistakes, and injuries (e.g., car accidents)
- Unacceptable sexual ideas (e.g., molestation)
- Unwanted violent impulses (e.g., to attack a helpless person)
- Unwanted sacrilegious thoughts (e.g., of desecrating a place of worship)
- Need for order, symmetry, and completeness
- Fears of certain numbers (e.g., 13, 666), colors (e.g., red), or words (e.g., murder)

Uncommon obsessions
- Fear of having an abortion without realizing it
- Fear that not being able to remember events means they didn't occur
- Fear that one's mind is contaminated by thoughts of unethical situations
- Fear of contamination from a geographic region.

> **Table 3**
> **Common and Uncommon Compulsive Rituals**
>
> **Common rituals**
> - Washing one's hands 40 times per day or taking multiple (lengthy) showers
> - Repeatedly cleaning objects or vacuuming the floor
> - Returning several times to check that the door is locked
> - Placing items in the "correct" order to achieve "balance"
> - Retracing one's steps
> - Rereading or rewriting to prevent mistakes
> - Calling relatives or "experts" to repeatedly ask for reassurance
> - Thinking the word "healthy" to counteract hearing the word "cancer"
> - Repeated and excessive confessing of one's "sins"
> - Repeating a prayer until it is said perfectly
>
> **Uncommon rituals**
> - Having to touch (with equal force) the right side of one's body after being touched on the left side
> - Having to look at certain points in space in a specified way
> - Having to mentally rearrange letters in sentences to spell out comforting words

1.2.1 Insight

People with OCD show a range of "insight" into the validity of their obsessions and compulsions – some acknowledge that their obsessions are unrealistic, while others are more firmly convinced (approaching delusional intensity) that the symptoms are rational. To accommodate this parameter of OCD, the DSM-5 includes specifiers to denote whether the person has (a) good or fair, (b) poor, or (c) no insight into the senselessness of their OCD symptoms. Often, the degree of insight varies within a person across time, situations, and across types of obsessions. For example, someone might have good insight into the senselessness of her violent obsessional thoughts, yet have poor insight regarding fears of contamination from chemicals.

Individuals vary in terms of their insight into the senselessness of their symptoms

1.2.2 Tics

DSM-5 also includes a specifier to distinguish between people with OCD with and without tic-like symptoms (or a history of a tic disorder). Whereas in "typical" OCD, obsessions lead to a negative *emotional* (affective) state such as anxiety or fear, "tic-related OCD" is characterized by a distressing *sensory* (somatic) state such as physical discomfort in specific body parts (e.g., face) or a diffuse psychological distress or tension (e.g., "in my head"). This sensory discomfort is relieved by motor responses (e.g., head twitching, eye blinking) that can be difficult to distinguish from tics as observed in Tourette's syndrome.

1.2.3   OCD From an Interpersonal Perspective

OCD commonly has an interpersonal component

The previous description highlights the experience of OCD from an individual perspective. Yet OCD commonly has an interpersonal component that may negatively impact close relationships, such as that with a parent, sibling, spouse, or romantic partner (Abramowitz et al., 2013). This component may be manifested in two ways. First, a partner or spouse (or other close friend or relative) might inadvertently be drawn to "help" or "accommodate" with performing compulsive rituals and avoidance behavior out of the desire to show care or concern for the sufferer (e.g., to help reduce expressions of anxiety). Second, OCD symptoms may lead to arguments and other forms of conflict within the relationships.

Symptom Accommodation

Accommodation occurs when a loved one (a) participates in the patient's rituals (e.g., answers reassurance-seeking questions, performs cleaning and checking behaviors for the patient), (b) helps with avoidance strategies (e.g., avoids places deemed "contaminated" by the patient), or (c) helps to resolve or minimize problems that have resulted from the patient's OCD symptoms (e.g., making excuses for the person's behavior, supplying money for special extra-strength soaps). Accommodation might occur at the request (or *demand*) of the individual with OCD, or it might be voluntary and based on the desire to show care and concern by reducing the OCD sufferer's distress. The following vignette illustrates accommodation:

> Mary had obsessional thoughts of harming her grandchildren and avoided her grandchildren and other stimuli that triggered violent images (e.g., knives, hammers, TV news programs). She insisted that her husband, Norman, refrain from discussing their grandchildren, hanging pictures of them in the house, and having them visit their home. Despite his reluctance, Norman went along with these wishes so that Mary could remain calm and avoid the obsessional thoughts. Norman said that, although it was a sacrifice, accommodating Mary's OCD symptoms was one way he showed her how much he loved and cared for her.

Accommodation can be subtle or overt (and extreme) and is observed in distressed and nondistressed relationships. Even if there is no obvious distress, accommodation creates a relationship "system" that fits with the OCD symptoms to perpetuate the problem. For example, accommodation might decrease a patient's motivation to engage in treatment that would require a great deal of effort and change the status quo. It might also be the chief way in which loved ones have learned to show affection for the OCD sufferer. Not surprisingly, accommodation is related to more severe OCD symptoms and poorer long-term treatment outcome.

Relationship Conflict

Relationships in which one person has OCD are often characterized by interdependency, unassertiveness, and avoidant communication patterns that foster conflict. Typically, OCD symptoms and interpersonal distress influence each other (rather than one exclusively leading to the other). For example, a father's contentious relationship with his adult daughter with OCD might contribute to anxiety and uncertainty that increases the daughter's obsessional doubting. Her compulsive reassurance seeking and overly cautious behavior might also lead to frequent disagreements and conflicts with her father.

1.3   Epidemiology

OCD has a 1-year prevalence of 1.2% and a lifetime prevalence of 2.3% in the adult population (this is equivalent to about 1 in 40 adults; Ruscio, Stein, Chiu, & Kessler, 2010). The disorder affects women slightly more often than men, and the age of onset, although earlier for males, is around age 19 on average.

Most individuals with OCD suffer for several years before receiving adequate diagnosis and treatment. Factors contributing to the under-recognition of OCD include the failure of patients to disclose symptoms, the failure of professionals to screen for obsessions and compulsions during mental status examinations, and difficulties with differential diagnoses (see Section 1.5).

1.4   Course and Prognosis

OCD symptoms typically develop gradually. An exception is the abrupt onset sometimes observed following pregnancy. The modal age of onset is 6–15 years in males and 20–29 years in females. Generally, OCD has a low rate of spontaneous remission. Left untreated, the disorder runs a chronic and deteriorating course, although symptoms may wax and wane in severity over time (often dependent upon levels of psychosocial stress).

> OCD generally runs a chronic and deteriorating course

1.5   Differential Diagnoses

In clinical practice, OCD can be difficult to differentiate from a number of problems with deceptively similar symptom patterns. Moreover, the terms "obsessive" and "compulsive" are often used indiscriminately to refer to phenomena that are not clinical obsessions and compulsions as defined by the DSM-5. This section highlights key differences between the symptoms of OCD and those of several other disorders.

> OCD is often confused with other disorders with seemingly similar features

1.5.1   Generalized Anxiety Disorder (GAD)

Anxious apprehension may be present in both OCD and GAD. However, whereas worries in GAD concern real-life problems (e.g., finances, relationships), obsessions in OCD contain senseless or bizarre content that is not about general life problems (e.g., fear of contracting AIDS from walking into a hospital) and often involve imagery. Moreover, the content of worries in

GAD may shift frequently, whereas the content of obsessional fears is generally stable over time.

1.5.2   Depression

OCD and depression both involve repetitive negative thoughts. However, depressive ruminations are generalized pessimistic ideas about the self, world, or future (e.g., "no one likes me") with frequent shifts in content. Unlike obsessions, ruminations are not strongly resisted and they do not elicit avoidance or compulsive rituals. Obsessions can be thoughts, ideas, images, and impulses that involve fears of specific disastrous consequences with infrequent shifts in content.

1.5.3   Tics and Tourette's Syndrome (TS)

Some individuals with OCD experience tic-like symptoms

Both OCD and TS sometimes involve stereotyped or rapid movements. However, tics (as in TS) are spontaneous acts evoked by a sensory urge. They serve to reduce sensory tension rather than as an escape from obsessive fear. By contrast, compulsions in OCD are deliberate acts evoked by affective distress and the urge to reduce fear.

1.5.4   Delusional Disorders (e.g., Schizophrenia)

Both OCD and delusional disorders involve bizarre, senseless, and fixed thoughts and beliefs. These thoughts might evoke affective distress in both conditions. However, unlike obsessions, delusions do not lead to compulsive rituals. Schizophrenia is also accompanied by other negative symptoms of thought disorders (e.g., loosening associations) that are not present in OCD.

1.5.5   Impulse Control Problems

Excessive and repetitive behaviors might be present in both OCD and in problems characterized by impulse control difficulties, such as pathological gambling, pathological shopping/buying, hair pulling disorder (aka trichotillomania), kleptomania, skin picking, compulsive Internet use (e.g., viewing pornography), and sexually impulsive behaviors. For this reason, some impulse control problems (i.e., skin picking and hair pulling) are now considered "obsessive-compulsive related disorders" in DSM-5. However, the repetitive behaviors in impulse control problems are typically performed to achieve a feeling of gratification (i.e., they are positively reinforced), whereas compulsive rituals in OCD are performed to escape from distress (i.e., they are negatively reinforced). Although individuals with impulse control problems may experience guilt, shame, and anxiety associated with their problematic behaviors, their anxiety is not triggered by obsessional cues as in OCD. That is, obsessions are not present. Thus, the treatment for these impulse control problems (i.e., habit reversal training) is very different than CBT for OCD.

1.5.6   Obsessive-Compulsive Personality Disorder (OCPD)

Whereas OCD and OCPD have overlapping names, there are more differences than similarities between the two conditions. OCPD is characterized by rigidity and inflexibility, meticulousness, and sometimes impulsive anger and hostility. People with OCPD often view these traits as functional and therefore consistent with their world view (i.e., they are "ego-syntonic"). On the other hand, OCD symptoms are experienced as upsetting and incongruent with the person's world view (i.e., "ego-dystonic"). Hence, OCD symptoms are resisted, whereas OCPD symptoms are not typically resisted because they do not cause personal distress (although others might become distressed over the person's behaviors).

1.5.7   Illness Anxiety (aka Hypochondriasis)

Persistent thoughts about illnesses and repetitive checking for reassurance can be present in both OCD and illness (or health-related) anxiety (hypochondriasis). In OCD, however, patients evidence additional obsessive themes (e.g., aggression, contamination), whereas in illness anxiety, patients are singly obsessed with their health.

1.5.8   Body Dysmorphic Disorder (BDD)

Both BDD (also an obsessive-compulsive related disorder) and OCD can involve intrusive, distressing thoughts concerning one's appearance. Moreover, repeated checking might be observed in both disorders. However, whereas people with OCD also have other obsessions, the focus of BDD symptoms is limited to one's appearance. In addition, the overall level of insight into the senselessness of BDD symptoms tends to be lower than for OCD.

1.5.9   Hoarding Disorder

Once considered a symptom of OCD, hoarding is now its own diagnostic entity (within the obsessive-compulsive related disorders) in DSM-5. The primary symptoms are excessive acquisition of large quantities of more or less useless objects (e.g., old newspapers and clothes) that cover the living areas of the home, and the inability or unwillingness to discard these objects even though they might impede activities such as cooking, cleaning, moving through the house, and sleeping. Although the collection of objects (and failure to discard them) can appear "compulsive" (and might sometimes be part of OCD-related checking rituals), hoarding behavior is typically not motivated by obsessional fear as in OCD.

> Hoarding is classified as its own disorder in DSM-5

1.6   Comorbidities

The most frequently co-occurring diagnoses among people with OCD are depressive and anxiety disorders. About 50% of people with OCD have experienced at least one major depressive episode (or dysthymia) in their lives. Commonly co-occurring anxiety disorders include generalized anxiety disorder, panic disorder, and social phobia, with rates ranging from 30 to 45% (Crino & Andrews, 1996a). When comorbid depression is present, OCD typically predates the depressive symptoms, suggesting that depressive symptoms usually occur in response to the distress and functional impairment associated with OCD (rather than as a precursor). Depressive symptoms also seem to be more strongly related to the severity of obsessions than to compulsions. Less frequently, individuals with OCD have comorbid eating disorders, tic disorders (e.g., Tourette's syndrome), and impulse control disorders. Studies generally agree that personality disorders belonging to the anxious cluster (e.g., obsessive-compulsive, avoidant) more commonly co-occur with OCD than those of other clusters (Crino & Andrews, 1996b).

1.7   Diagnostic Procedures and Documentation

This section reviews the empirically established structured and semi-structured diagnostic interviews and self-report measures for assessing the presence and severity of OCD symptoms, as well as for documenting changes in these symptoms during a course of psychological treatment.

1.7.1   Structured Diagnostic Interviews

Two structured diagnostic interviews that are based on DSM-IV-TR criteria can be used to confirm the diagnosis of DSM-5 OCD (since very little changed with respect to the diagnostic criteria): the Anxiety Disorders Interview Schedule for DSM-IV (ADIS-IV; Di Nardo, Brown, & Barlow, 1994) and the Structured Clinical Interview for DSM-IV (SCID-IV; First, Spitzer, Gibbon, & Williams, 2002). Both of these instruments possess good reliability and validity. The SCID is available over the Internet at http://www.scid4.org, and the ADIS is available from Oxford University Press.

1.7.2   Semi-Structured Symptom Interviews

OCD is unique among the psychological disorders in that the form and content of its symptoms can vary widely from one person to the next. In fact, two individuals with OCD might present with completely nonoverlapping symptoms. Such heterogeneity necessitates a thorough assessment of the *topography* of the individual's symptoms: What types of obsessions and compulsions are present and how severe are these symptoms?

Yale-Brown Obsessive Compulsive Scale (Y-BOCS)

The Y-BOCS (Goodman, Price, Rasmussen, Mazure, Delgado et al., 1989; Goodman, Price, Rasmussen, Mazure, Fleischmann et al., 1989), which includes a symptom checklist and a severity rating scale, is ideal for addressing these questions. Between 30 and 60 min might be required to administer this semi-structured interview. A full copy of the measure appears on a Wikipedia page for the Y-BOCS. The first part of the symptom checklist provides definitions and examples of obsessions and compulsions that the clinician reads to the patient. Next, the clinician reviews a comprehensive list of over 50 common obsessions and compulsions and asks the patient whether each symptom is currently present or has occurred in the past. Finally, the most prominent obsessions, compulsions, and OCD-related avoidance behaviors are listed.

One limitation of the Y-BOCS symptom checklist is that it assesses obsessions and compulsions according to *form* rather than *function*. It is therefore up to the clinician to inquire about the relationship between obsessions and compulsions (i.e., which obsessional thoughts evoke which rituals). A second limitation is that the checklist contains only one item assessing mental rituals. Thus, the clinician must probe in a less structured way for the presence of these covert symptoms. The assessment of mental rituals is discussed further in Section 4.1.1.

The Y-BOCS Severity Scale includes ten items to assess the following five parameters of obsessions (items 1–5) and compulsions (items 6–10): (a) time, (b) interference, (c) distress, (d) efforts to resist, and (e) perceived control. Each item is rated on a scale from 0 to 4, and the item scores are summed to produce a total score ranging from 0 (no symptoms) to 40 (extreme). Table 4 shows the clinical breakdown of scores on the Y-BOCS severity scale. The measure has acceptable reliability, validity, and sensitivity to change. An advantage of the Y-BOCS is that it assesses OCD symptom severity independent of symptom content. However, a drawback of this approach is that the clinician must be cautious to avoid rating the symptoms of other problems (e.g., GAD, impulse control problems) as obsessions or compulsions.

The Y-BOCS – a measure of OCD symptom severity

Table 4
Clinical Breakdown of Scores on the Y-BOCS Severity Scale

Y-BOCS score	Clinical severity
0–7	Subclinical
8–15	Mild
16–23	Moderate
24–31	Severe
32–40	Extreme

Brown Assessment of Beliefs Scale (BABS)

Since poor insight has been linked to attenuated treatment outcome, the assessment of OCD should include determination of the extent to which the patient perceives his or her obsessions and compulsions as senseless and excessive.

The BABS – a measure of insight in OCD

The BABS (Eisen et al., 1998) is a semi-structured interview that contains seven items and assesses insight as a continuous variable. The patient first identifies one or two current obsessional fears (e.g., "If I touch dirty laundry without washing my hands, I will become sick"). Next, individual items assess (a) conviction in this belief, (b) perceptions of how others view this belief, (c) explanation for why others hold a different view, (d) willingness to challenge the belief, (e) attempts to disprove the belief, (f) insight into the senselessness of the belief, and (g) ideas/delusions of reference. Each item is rated on a scale from 0 to 4, and the first six items are summed to obtain a total score of 0 to 24 (higher scores indicate poorer insight). The seventh item is not included in the total score. The BABS has good reliability, validity, and sensitivity to change. It is available on the Internet at: http://www.veale.co.uk/wp-content/uploads/2010/11/BABS_revised_501.pdf.

1.7.3 Self-Report Inventories

Self-report inventories are used to gather additional severity data

Psychometrically validated self-report questionnaires can be used to supplement the clinical interviews described above. Such questionnaires are easily administered, carefully worded, and have well-established norms. Accordingly, they are best used to corroborate information obtained from clinical interviewing and to monitor symptom severity during treatment.

Dimensional Obsessive-Compulsive Scale (DOCS)

The DOCS – a brief measure of OCD severity

The DOCS is a 20-item self-report measure that assesses the severity of the four most consistently identified OCD symptom dimensions, which correspond to the measure's four subscales: (a) contamination, (b) responsibility for harm and mistakes, (c) symmetry/ordering/incompleteness, and (d) unacceptable/taboo obsessions. Each subscale begins with a description of the symptom dimension along with examples of representative obsessions and rituals. The examples clarify the form and function of each dimension's fundamental obsessional fears, compulsive rituals, and avoidance behaviors. Each subscale contains five items (rated 0 to 4) to assess the following parameters of severity: (a) time occupied by obsessions and rituals, (b) avoidance behavior, (c) associated distress, (d) functional interference, and (e) difficulty disregarding the obsessions and refraining from the compulsions. Scores for each subscale (symptom dimension) range from 0 (minimum) to 20 (maximum). The DOCS subscales have excellent reliability, and validity, and sensitivity to treatment effects (Abramowitz et al., 2010). Total scores of at least 18 and 21 can help distinguish people with OCD from those with no disorder and an anxiety disorder, respectively. The DOCS is freely available on the Internet at http://www.jabramowitz.com/resources-and-free-stuff.html.

1.7.4 Documenting Changes in Symptom Levels

Assessing OCD symptoms throughout treatment

Continual assessment of OCD and related symptoms throughout the course of psychological treatment assists the clinician in evaluating treatment response. It is not enough to simply assume that "he seems to be less obsessed," or "it looks like she has cut down on her compulsions," or even for the patient to report that he or she now "feels better." We recommend periodic assessment and comparison with baseline symptom levels using psychometrically validated self-report and interview measures to clarify objectively in what ways treatment has been helpful and what work remains to be done.

2

Theories and Models

A number of theories have been proposed to explain the development and clinical picture of OCD. This chapter reviews several theoretical models that have been well-studied, with an emphasis on the cognitive-behavioral model which forms the basis of the treatment program described in Chapter 4.

2.1   Biological Theories

2.1.1   Neurotransmitter Theories

Biological theories of OCD

Biological models of OCD can be categorized into neurotransmitter and neuroanatomical theories. Prevailing neurotransmitter theories propose that abnormalities in the serotonin system, particularly the hypersensitivity of postsynaptic serotonergic receptors, underlie OCD symptoms. This "serotonin hypothesis" was proposed following observations that serotonergic medication, but not other kinds of antidepressants, were effective in reducing OCD symptoms. However, results from numerous studies that have directly examined the relationship between serotonin and OCD have been inconsistent. For instance, some studies report increased concentrations of serotonin metabolites in the cerebrospinal fluid of OCD patients relative to nonpatients; other studies do not report such findings. Whereas the preferential response of OCD to serotonergic medication is often championed as supporting the serotonin hypothesis, this argument is of little value since the hypothesis was derived from this treatment outcome result. To date there are few convincing data to suggest that problems with serotonin functioning (or other neurotransmitters) mediate OCD symptoms.

2.1.2   Neuroanatomical Theories

Predominant neuroanatomical models of OCD propose that obsessions and compulsions arise from structural and functional abnormalities in particular areas of the brain, specifically the orbitofrontal-subcortical circuits. These circuits are thought to connect regions of the brain involved in processing information with those involved in the initiation of certain behavioral responses; and their over activity is thought to lead to OCD. Neuroanatomic models have been derived from imaging studies in which activity levels in specific parts of the brain is compared between OCD patients and healthy controls. For example, positron emission tomography (PET) studies have consistently found increased glucose utilization in the orbitofrontal cortex (OFC) among patients with OCD as compared to nonpatients.

Although thought-provoking, neuroanatomical studies are cross-sectional and correlational, and therefore cannot address hypotheses about cause, such as whether OCD arises from apparent dysfunctions in the brain, or whether the observed alterations in brain function represent normally functioning brain systems that are simply affected by the presence of chronic obsessional anxiety; thus, the direction of causality remains unclear. Moreover, to date there is no biological (i.e., neurochemical, neuroanatomical, or genetic) test for OCD.

2.2 Psychological Theories

2.2.1 Learning Theory

Early learning (conditioning) models of OCD were drawn from Mowrer's (1960) two-factor theory which proposes that pathological fear is acquired by classical conditioning and maintained by operant conditioning. For example, an obsessional fear of cemeteries is thought to arise from a traumatic experience during which anxiety becomes associated with such places. This fear is then maintained by behaviors that prevent the natural extinction of the fear, such as avoidance of cemeteries and funeral homes, and compulsive praying. Avoidance and rituals are negatively reinforced by the immediate (albeit temporary) reduction in discomfort that they engender. Thus, such behaviors develop into strong habits.

A learning (conditioning) model

Research supports some aspects of the learning theory, but not others. For example, obsessional stimuli indeed *evoke* anxiety, and compulsive rituals do bring about an immediate *reduction* in anxiety and distress. However, traumatic conditioning experiences do not appear to be necessary for the development of obsessions. Contemporary cognitive-behavioral models (as described in Section 2.2.3) were subsequently formulated to explain the development of obsessional fear.

2.2.2 Cognitive Deficit Models

Because people with OCD sometimes demonstrate the appearance of reduced performance on cognitive tasks such as executive functioning, cognitive inhibition, and some forms of memory, some theorists have proposed that OCD is characterized by deficits in neuropsychological and information-processing functioning. However, such impairment, if present at all, tends to be mild and of trivial clinical importance (Abramovitch, Abramowitz, & Mittleman, 2013). Moreover, these minor deficits could be caused by the effects of anxiety and fear which characterize OCD (as opposed to the other way around). Cognitive deficit models have two key limitations. First, they do not account for the heterogeneity of OCD symptoms (e.g., why some patients have contamination

Cognitive deficit models

obsessions and others have sexual obsessions). Second, because mild cognitive deficits are present in many psychological disorders (e.g., panic disorder, bulimia nervosa), these models fail to explain why such deficits give rise to OCD instead of one of these other disorders. Thus, if cognitive deficits play a causal role in OCD at all, they most likely represent a nonspecific vulnerability factor. Additionally, an alternative explanation is that people with OCD have reduced *confidence* in their memory and other cognitive functions.

2.2.3 Contemporary Cognitive-Behavioral Models

Cognitive-behavioral approaches to OCD, which serve as the basis for the treatment program described in this book, begin with the well-established finding that intrusive thoughts (i.e., thoughts, images, and impulses that intrude into consciousness) are normal experiences that most people have from time to time. Sometimes triggered by external stimuli (e.g., thoughts of contamination that are triggered by the sight of a garbage truck), such intrusions usually reflect themes that are of importance to the person (e.g., religion and morality, loved ones, health and safety, etc.). Research also shows that people with no history of OCD have similar types of intrusive thoughts about "taboo" topics such as sex, violence, blasphemy, and germs.

Contemporary cognitive-behavioral models of OCD form the basis for CBT

The cognitive-behavioral model proposes that normal intrusions develop into highly distressing and time-consuming clinical obsessions when the person mistakenly appraises such intrusions as threatening, personally significant, or as provoking uncertainty that the person perceives as unmanageable or intolerable. For example, consider the unwanted thought of verbally abusing a beloved elderly family member. Most people would consider such an intrusion as meaningless or harmless (e.g., "mental noise"). However, according to the cognitive-behavioral model, such an intrusion would develop into a clinical obsession if the person attaches to it a high degree of importance and uncertainty, leading to an escalation in negative emotion; for example, "Thinking about verbally abusing Grand-pop means I'm a terrible person who must be extra careful to make sure I don't lose control." Such appraisals evoke distress and motivate the person to try to (a) control, suppress, or neutralize the unwanted thought (e.g., by praying or replacing it with a "safe" thought), (b) attempt to prevent any harmful events associated with the intrusion (e.g., by avoiding elderly people), or (c) gain certainty regarding any possible feared consequences (e.g., seeking reassurance).

Compulsive rituals are conceptualized as efforts to control or reduce obsessional distress and anxiety, remove unwanted intrusions, and gain certainty that feared consequences will not occur. However, rituals are counterproductive for a number of reasons. First, because they are sometimes "effective" in providing the desired reduction in distress in the short-term, these strategies are negatively reinforced and frequently evolve into time-consuming patterns that impair functioning and quality of life. Second, because they provide an immediate (albeit fleeting) escape from anxiety and doubt, rituals prevent the person from learning that thoughts, anxiety, and uncertainty are manageable. Third, rituals prevent the person from learning that obsessional distress eventually abates naturally when feared situations are confronted for extended periods of time. Fourth, rituals lead to an increase in the frequency of obsessions by serving as reminders of obsessional intrusions, thereby triggering their recurrence. For example, compulsively checking the stove can trigger intrusions about house fires. Attempts at distracting oneself from unwanted intrusions may paradoxically increase the frequency of intrusions, possibly because the distractors become reminders (retrieval cues) of the intrusions. Finally, performing rituals preserves dysfunctional beliefs and misinterpretations of obsessional thoughts. That is, when feared consequences do not occur after performance of a ritual, the person (erroneously) attributes this to the ritual that was performed, rather than (correctly) to the innocuousness of the intrusion.

To summarize, when a person appraises an otherwise normally occurring mental intrusion as threatening and personally significant, he or she becomes distressed and attempts to control or remove the intrusion, reduce uncertainty, and prevent the feared consequences. This paradoxically increases the frequency of intrusions. Thus, the intrusions escalate into persistent and distressing clinical obsessions to which the person becomes exquisitely sensitive. Because the obsessional thought is experienced as distressing, it evokes urges to perform some response – overt or covert – to neutralize the distress and bring about assurance of safety. Compulsions maintain the intrusions and prevent the self-correction of mistaken (catastrophic) appraisals and the belief that one cannot manage with the associated anxiety and uncertainty. Table 5 summarizes the various factors that maintain OCD symptoms.

Brief summary of the cognitive-behavioral approach to OCD

Factors that maintain obsessional fear

Table 5
Summary of Maintenance Processes in OCD

Maintenance process	Description
Selective attention	Hypervigilance for threat cues enhances the detection of obsessional stimuli.
Physiological factors	The fight-or-flight response is a normal response to perceived threat. Emotional reasoning reaffirms mistaken beliefs that lead to feeling anxious.
Anxiety-reduction behaviors	Overt and covert rituals, reassurance-seeking, and neutralizing strategies are reinforced by the immediate reduction in distress they engender. In the long-term, these strategies prevent disconfirmation of mistaken beliefs because of how their outcomes are incorrectly interpreted.
Passive avoidance	Avoidance produces temporary anxiety reduction, but prevents disconformation of overestimates of risk because the person never has the opportunity to find out that danger is unlikely.
Concealment of obsessions	Hiding obsessions from others prevents disconfirmation of mistaken beliefs about the normalcy of intrusive thoughts.
Attempted thought control	Attempts to control or suppress unwanted thoughts lead to an increase in unwanted thoughts. Misappraisal of thought control failure leads to further distress.

Misinterpretations of one's thoughts might include any appraisal of the intrusive thought as personally significant or threatening. An example is the belief that thinking about bad behavior is morally equivalent to performing the corresponding behavior (e.g., "Thinking about molesting a child is as bad as actually doing it"). An international group of researchers interested in the cognitive basis of OCD, the Obsessive Compulsive Cognitions Working Group (OCCWG; Frost & Steketee, 2002) identified three domains of "core beliefs" thought to underlie the development of obsessions from normal intrusive thoughts. These are summarized in Table 6. Figure 1 graphically depicts the contemporary cognitive-behavioral conceptual model. It is important to point out that, like the other models, questions remain regarding the cognitive-behavioral approach. Although research consistently supports the tenants of this model in general, cognitive and behavioral factors do not account completely for OCD symptoms, and it is likely that there are other factors involved in the development and maintenance of the problem.

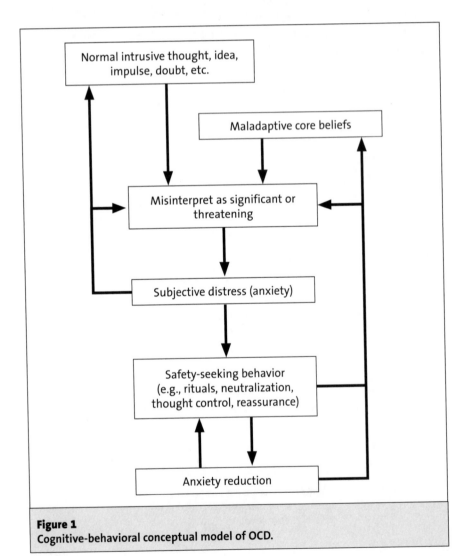

Figure 1
Cognitive-behavioral conceptual model of OCD.

Table 6
Domains of Pathogenic Beliefs in OCD

Belief	Description
Inflated responsibility/ Overestimation of threat	Belief that one has the power to cause and/ or the duty to prevent negative outcomes featured in intrusive thoughts.
	Belief that negative events associated with intrusive thoughts are likely and would be insufferable.
Exaggeration of the importance of thoughts and need to control thoughts	Belief that the mere presence of a thought indicates that the thought is significant.
	Belief that complete control over one's thoughts is both necessary and possible.
Perfectionism/intolerance of uncertainty	Belief that mistakes and imperfection are intolerable.
	Belief that it is necessary and possible to be 100% certain that negative outcomes will not occur.

Implications of the Cognitive-Behavioral Model

Normalizing Effects

The cognitive-behavioral approach provides a logically and empirically consistent account of OCD symptoms that assumes the presence of intact learning (conditioning) processes and normally functioning (albeit maladaptive) cognitive processes. There is no appeal to "chemical imbalances" or broken brain parts to explain OCD symptoms. Even the maladaptive beliefs and assumptions that lead to obsessions are viewed as "mistakes" and "biases" rather than "disease processes." Furthermore, avoidance and compulsive rituals to reduce perceived threat and uncertainty would be considered adaptive if harm was indeed likely. However, OCD patients' obsessive fears are exaggerated. Therefore, their avoidance and safety-seeking rituals are not only irrational, but highly problematic since they perpetuate a vicious cycle of intrusion –> misappraisal –> anxiety that causes a reduction in quality of life.

> The cognitive-behavioral approach assumes no specific brain dysfunction

Vulnerability to OCD

The distal cause of OCD is unknown, but the problem's etiology probably involves interactions among (as yet not well-understood) biological and genetic factors and environmental variables. Cognitive-behavioral models propose that certain experiences lead people to develop core beliefs that underlie OCD. For example, an obsession could develop in someone who was taught high moral standards and expected to obey rigid and extreme codes of conduct where the threat of punishment for disobedience was constantly present (e.g., as in certain strict religious doctrines). However, empirical evidence supporting the role of these kinds of experiences in the etiology of OCD is equivocal.

Treatment Implications of the Model

**Treatment
implications of the
cognitive-behavioral
model**

The cognitive-behavioral model identifies specific targets for reducing OCD symptoms. In particular, effective treatment must help patients (a) correct maladaptive beliefs and appraisals that lead to obsessional fear and (b) decrease avoidance and safety-seeking behaviors (e.g., rituals) that prevent the self-correction of maladaptive beliefs. In short, the task of cognitive-behavior therapy (CBT) is to foster an evaluation of obsessional stimuli (situations, stimuli, thoughts, and internal sensations) as acceptably low risk (although not 100% safe) and therefore not demanding of further action, such as rituals, the need to reduce anxiety, or gain certainty about feared consequences. Patients must come to understand their problem not in terms of the risk of feared consequences, but in terms of how they are thinking and behaving in response to stimuli that objectively pose a low risk (i.e., not more than everyday risk) of harm. Those with aggressive obsessions must view their problem as lending too much significance to meaningless intrusive thoughts (instead of how they are going to achieve the ultimate guarantee that they will never harm anyone). Patients with washing rituals must see their problem not as needing a sure-fire way to eliminate all germs, but as the need to change how they evaluate and respond to situations that realistically pose a low risk of illness. The treatment procedures outlined in Chapter 4 are derived from the learning and cognitive-behavioral models of OCD, and therefore address these targets.

3

Diagnosis and Treatment Indications

This chapter provides a framework for conducting a diagnostic assessment and providing consultation regarding the treatment of OCD. The cognitive-behavioral model and its treatment implications (see Chapter 2) determine how information about the patient's symptoms is assessed and conceptualized. The initial consultation provides an excellent opportunity to initiate rapport building and begin socializing the patient to the cognitive-behavioral approach.

3.1   Form vs. Function

Whereas the diagnostic criteria for OCD emphasize descriptions of obsessions and compulsions, the cognitive-behavioral model emphasizes the *functional* aspects of these phenomena. From this perspective, the essential features of OCD are anxiety-evoking obsessional thoughts and anxiety-reducing strategies such as rituals and avoidance. It is the person's intolerance of uncertainty and other dysfunctional beliefs and appraisals of obsessional stimuli which give rise to obsessional fear. Thus, it is important to assess how the patient gives meaning to obsessional stimuli. Whereas "compulsiveness" and repetition might be the most outwardly observable signs of OCD, patients actually deploy a variety of escape and avoidance behaviors in response to obsessional distress, and only some of these behaviors are repetitive or "compulsive." Table 7 shows the array of "safety behaviors" that might be observed in OCD.

> The cognitive-behavioral model emphasizes *functional* aspects of OCD symptoms

Table 7
Types of Safety Behaviors Observed in OCD

Type	Examples
Passive avoidance	Avoidance of situations and stimuli (e.g., driving, being the last one to leave the house, toilets, "666")
Compulsive rituals	Hand washing, checking, seeking reassurance, repeating routine activities
Covert neutralizing	Mental rituals (e.g., repeating prayers, "good" words, or "safe" phrases), brief mental acts (e.g., canceling out a "bad" thought with a "good" thought)
Brief or subtle "mini" rituals	Use of wipes or paper towels, quick checks of appliances, scrutinizing others' behavior or facial expressions

Table 8
Common OCD Symptom Presentations

Presentation	Commonly observed symptoms
Contamination	Obsessions concerning contamination from dirt, germs, body secretions, household items, poisonous materials; washing and cleaning rituals, avoidance
Harming	Obsessions concerning responsibility for injury or harm to others; compulsive checking, seeking reassurance, repeating activities to prevent disasters
Incompleteness	Obsessions concerning order, asymmetry, imbalance (perhaps the fear that discomfort will persist indefinitely); compulsive arranging, ordering, repeating
Unacceptable thoughts	Obsessional thoughts, impulses, images of sex, sacrilege, and violence; mental rituals, neutralizing, seeking reassurance

It is also important to assess how the patient's safety behaviors are related to obsessional stimuli and dysfunctional thinking patterns.

Research indicates the presence of OCD symptom dimensions involving specific types of obsessions and rituals or safety behaviors (McKay et al., 2004). Table 8 shows the most commonly identified OCD symptom dimensions. There is often an overlap among the presentations.

3.2   The Diagnostic Assessment

How to conduct a diagnostic assessment for OCD

The diagnostic interview begins with the patient providing a general description of his or her problem, the effects on functioning and quality of life, as well as the reasons for seeking help. Be sure to ascertain the functional relationship between obsessions and rituals as described in previous sections. Also, determine the onset, historical course of the problem, social, developmental, and medical history, and personal/family history of psychiatric treatment, along with substance use (i.e., drugs, alcohol, tobacco), and exercise and sleep habits. In addition, assess the treatment history (particularly treatment for OCD) as this may influence your current recommendations. Once this information has been obtained, use the Y-BOCS, BABS, and DOCS to gather additional severity data. We also recommend assessing depressive symptoms.

Two additional self-report instruments, the Obsessional Beliefs Questionnaire (OBQ) and the Interpretations of Intrusions Inventory (III) (Obsessive Compulsive Cognitions Working Group, 2005), can be administered to assess OCD-related dysfunctional beliefs (i.e., those described in Table 6). The OBQ and III are reprinted in Frost and Steketee's (2002) edited volume on cognitive aspects of OCD.

Clinical Pearl
When Patients Report Obsessions or Compulsions in Isolation

Whereas the majority of OCD patients readily describe both obsessional fears and compulsive rituals, some present with complaints of "pure obsessions" or "compulsions without obsessions." When assessing such patients, keep in mind that greater than 90% of people with OCD report both obsessions and compulsions. Thus, you might need to conduct a more in-depth assessment. For individuals reporting only obsessions, this means inquiring about the use of any anxiety-reduction strategy (mental rituals or subtle behavioral or cognitive neutralizing or avoidance) that might be functioning to maintain obsessional fear. Most patients don't recognize these safety behaviors as OCD symptoms, or might confuse mental rituals and obsessions, but these mental rituals maintain obsessional fear just as surely as overt rituals. If these phenomena are not present, perhaps the "obsessions" are not intrusive or anxiety-evoking and therefore not indicative of OCD (e.g., perhaps they are depressive ruminations, worries as in GAD, or other ego-syntonic thoughts).

When patients describe compulsive behaviors but fail to define obsessional fear, inquire about what triggers these behaviors. If they are not evoked by specific intrusive or distressing thoughts or situations as described in Chapter 1, OCD might not be the correct diagnosis. Perhaps an impulse-control (e.g., trichotillomania) or tic disorder is present. You can use the Y-BOCS checklist, self-report questionnaires, and detailed inquiry regarding the functional aspects of reported symptoms to rule in or rule out the diagnosis of OCD.

3.3   Identifying the Appropriate Treatment

3.3.1   Empirically Supported Treatments for OCD

Practice guidelines for the treatment of OCD (which can be found online at http://www.psychiatryonline.org) include two empirically supported treatments: CBT involving ERP and pharmacotherapy involving serotonin reuptake inhibitor (SRI) medication. This section briefly describes these treatments and their advantages and disadvantages.

Empirically supported treatments for OCD

Medication for OCD

Table 9 displays the brand names, generic names, and therapeutic doses of medications studied using randomized controlled trials for OCD. These agents are thought to reduce OCD by increasing the concentration of serotonin. On average, SRIs produce a 20–40% improvement in OCD symptoms over a 12-week period for most people with OCD. There are various advantages and disadvantages to using SRI medication for treating OCD.

Advantages of Medication:
- Generally safe and easy to use
- Clinically effective: 20–40% symptom reduction on average for most people with OCD

Disadvantages of Medication:
- Limited improvement rates
- A substantial minority of patients show little or no response
- Possibility of side effects
- Must be used continuously in order to sustain any improvement

Table 9
Medications With Demonstrated Efficacy for Treating OCD*

Brand name	Generic name	Therapeutic dose
Anafranil	Clomipramine	Up to 250 mg/day
Zoloft	Sertraline	Up to 200 mg/day
Prozac	Fluoxetine	40–80 mg/day
Luvox	Fluvoxamine	Up to 300 mg/day
Paxil	Paroxetine	40–60 mg/day
Celexa	Citalopram	Up to 60 mg/day

* At least one double-blind randomized controlled trial exists in which the medication was more effective than a placebo.

Cognitive-Behavior Therapy for OCD

CBT is a multicomponent approach based on an understanding of how OCD symptoms are *maintained* (rather than its putative *causes*). The psychoeducational component entails socializing the patient to the cognitive-behavioral model and providing an explanation of the individual treatment techniques and how they work (i.e., the treatment rationale). Cognitive techniques for OCD involve rational discussion to help the patient identify and correct mistaken beliefs that underlie obsessional fears, avoidance, and safety-seeking behaviors.

Exposure and response prevention are the centerpiece of CBT for OCD. *Exposure* entails confronting situations and thoughts that evoke obsessive fear. This is often accompanied by imagining the feared consequences of exposure. For example, an individual who fears contamination and sickness from garbage cans would practice touching garbage cans and then imagine being contaminated with germs and coming down with an illness. The procedure involves the patient remaining exposed to the feared situation, without performing compulsive rituals or safety behaviors, and observing that feared consequences are unlikely and that he or she can manage the associated distress and uncertainty evoked during the exposure. Thus the *response prevention* component of CBT entails refraining from any behaviors (behavioral and mental rituals, subtle avoidance, and reassurance-seeking) that serve to reduce obsessional anxiety or terminate exposure. For example, the patient described above would refrain from cleaning rituals.

Exposure and response prevention facilitate extinction of obsessional fear by helping the patient develop new learning that obsessional cues are generally safe and manageable. This new learning competes with existing fear-based associations. When CBT/ERP is carried out in certain ways that we illustrate in Chapter 4, the new learning inhibits the older fear-based associations (i.e., maximizing inhibitory learning) and the patient recognizes that obsessional fears are excessive and that rituals are not necessary to prevent disasters or reduce distress.

As with medication treatment, there are advantages and disadvantages to CBT.

> **Exposure and response prevention are the centerpiece of CBT**

Advantages of CBT
- Clinically effective: 60–70% symptom reduction on average
- Treatment is fairly brief (usually 15–20 sessions)
- Long-term maintenance of treatment gains

Disadvantages of CBT
- Patient must work hard to achieve improvement
- Involves purposely evoking anxiety during exposure
- Not widely available due to a relative lack of well-trained clinicians

3.4   Factors That Influence Treatment Decisions

This section considers factors that influence clinical decisions regarding which type of treatment to recommend for a particular individual with OCD.

> **Factors that influence decisions about treatment**

3.4.1   Age

CBT is the treatment of choice for all age groups with OCD. Compared to young and middle-aged adults, children and the elderly tend to have more difficulty with adherence to medication. The elderly are more vulnerable to drug side effects due to reduced metabolic rate and possible interactions with other medicines. Family conflict can interfere with CBT in children.

3.4.2   Gender

Men and women respond equally well to CBT. However, some patients feel more comfortable with a therapist of the same sex, especially if sexual or contamination concerns are present (e.g., fears of touching one's genitals). A same-sex therapist would also be preferable to accompany patients during exposure to public restrooms.

3.4.3   Ethnic/Racial Background

Some members of minority groups are uncomfortable receiving psychological treatments and prefer pharmacotherapy over CBT, as the former carries less stigma. Such individuals might be less willing to report symptoms to a therapist from a different ethnoracial background. Despite these issues, many minority patients with OCD achieve clinically significant improvement with CBT (Williams, Chambless, & Steketee, 1998).

3.4.4   Educational Level

Successful CBT requires that the patient grasp a theoretical model of OCD and a rationale for treatment. Patients must also be able to implement challenging treatment procedures on their own and consolidate information learned during exposure exercises. These tasks may be difficult for individuals who are very concrete in their thinking. Medication might be recommended for developmentally disabled and cognitively impaired patients.

3.4.5   Patient Preference

Patient preference should be considered

Preference for a particular treatment modality should be considered. Reviewing the advantages and disadvantages of each approach allows the patent to make an informed decision about which therapy they would prefer to receive. Greater adherence to either treatment (especially CBT) can be expected from patients who agree willingly to a particular plan, as opposed to those situations in which treatment is forced on them.

3.4.6   Clinical Presentation

ERP targets obsessions and compulsions. Thus, if such symptoms are not primary complaints, ERP is not recommended. Because ERP requires a substantial commitment, it should not be initiated when patients are concurrently engaged in therapies likely to compete for time and energy.

In general, OCD symptom severity should not factor into the decision of whether to treat patients with medication or CBT – we suggest CBT as the first line treatment for any severity level. However, severe symptoms may require a more intense regimen of whatever treatment is offered: i.e., a higher dose of medicine or more frequent CBT sessions. If the patient presents a danger to self or others, inpatient treatment is recommended. Where possible, however, we recommend CBT be conducted on an outpatient basis to maximize generalizability of treatment gains to the patient's own personal surroundings.

3.4.7   OCD Symptom Theme

Both CBT and medication can produce improvement across the various presentations of OCD (e.g., washing, checking). Although it is clinical lore that patients with obsessions and mental rituals (sometimes referred to as "pure obsessionals") do not fare well in CBT, as we show in Chapter 4, ERP can indeed be adapted to successfully treat this presentation of OCD.

3.4.8   Interpersonal Factors

Accommodation of OCD symptoms by a partner, relative, or close friend is related to more severe obsessions and compulsions as well as to poorer long-term treatment outcome. Similarly, interpersonal communication patterns characterized by criticism, hostility, and emotional over-involvement are associated with premature treatment discontinuation and symptom relapse. On the other hand, communication patterns characterized by empathy, hopefulness, and assertiveness are associated with successful outcomes with CBT. Where accommodation and/or hostility are present, it is worth considering involving the partner or a family member in treatment in order to work on modifying these maladaptive communication patterns that maintain OCD symptoms. Before enlisting such a "treatment buddy," be sure he or she can interact in a supportive yet firm (i.e., assertive) way with the patient. The ability to be firm, relaxed, and empathic is predictive of better results. Emotional over-involvement, hostility, and inconsistent behavior can lead to treatment attrition.

> **Consider involving a partner or family member in treatment**

3.4.9   Insight

Patients with poorer insight into the senselessness of their OCD symptoms show an attenuated response to CBT due to (a) reluctance to engage in ERP and (b) difficulty consolidating what is to be learned from exposure. While CBT is worth attempting, increased use of cognitive therapy techniques might be necessary to help patients engage in (and benefit from) exposure tasks. Another augmentative approach is to use medication; some psychiatrists use antipsychotic medication to treat patients with very poor insight.

3.4.10   Comorbidity

OCD patients with comorbid depression and comorbid GAD show reduced response to CBT. Seriously depressed patients become demoralized and have trouble complying with treatment instructions. Their strong negative affect may also exacerbate OCD symptoms. In GAD, pervasive worry detracts from patients' mental resources available for learning skills in CBT for OCD.

Other conditions likely to interfere with CBT are those that involve alterations in perception, cognition, and judgment, such as psychotic and manic symptoms. Patients actively abusing psychoactive substances are also poor CBT candidates. These problems impede the ability to profit from CBT exercises and can also reduce adherence. Bringing these comorbid conditions under control is a requirement before beginning CBT.

Both CBT and medication may be adversely affected by severe personality disorder (PD) psychopathology. Anxious (e.g., OCPD) and dramatic (e.g., histrionic) traits may interfere with rapport development; yet, success is possible if a therapeutic relationship can be established. Patients with personality traits in the odd cluster (e.g., schizotypy) present a challenge to CBT due to interpersonal factors and their reduced ability to consolidate corrective information from exposure or cognitive interventions.

3.4.11 Treatment History

Patients who have received an adequate dosage of one or more SRIs for a reasonable length of time (at least 8–10 weeks) without a response are generally unlikely to respond to other SRIs, or to combinations of SRIs. Thus, for medicated patients who have not had psychological treatment, CBT is the logical recommendation. If patients report that they have undergone CBT, assess the adequacy of the previous trial before making additional recommendations. If therapy sessions were infrequent, or if therapist-guided exposure was not incorporated, a course of adequate CBT should be considered. On the other hand, a history of adherence problems may suggest the need for residential treatment or a supportive approach.

3.5   Presenting the Recommendation for CBT

How to recommend CBT to the patient

Once you have determined that a patient is a candidate for CBT, present him or her with a summary of the assessment results and a rationale for starting treatment. At the patient's discretion, close friends or family members (e.g., spouse, partner, or parent) who can be counted on to provide support can be included in this discussion. Convey the following points during this consultation.

- Review the data collected during the interview which suggest the presence (and severity level) of OCD.
- Define OCD and review the signs and symptoms as discussed in Section 1.1. Use the patient's own symptoms as examples. Emphasize that OCD is a chronic problem that is unlikely to get better without effective treatment.
- Tell the patient that the exact causes of OCD are unknown and that, most likely, numerous factors (biological and environmental) contribute to its development.
- Convey that effective treatment does not require that we know the *causes*, but that we understand the *symptoms* of OCD and how they work. Fortunately, after much research, we understand these symptoms very well. Treatment is based on our understanding of these symptoms.
- Describe CBT as a form of treatment in which the patient learns skills to (a) more effectively manage fear-provoking situations and unwanted obsessional thoughts, (b) reduce avoidance behavior and compulsive rituals, and (c) improve quality of life.
- Using the information in Section 3.3.1 as a guide, describe the ERP procedures. Provide examples of the kinds of exposure exercises and response prevention strategies that might be used in treatment.
- Explain that during treatment the patient can expect to become anxious, but that through lots of practice, he or she will learn how to manage this anxiety in better ways. Additional ways to convey this might include: "You will learn how to have a healthier relationship with your own thoughts and feelings" and "The object of treatment is not so much to make anxiety go away forever, which is impossible, but

rather to be 'better' at having anxiety when it does occur." Put another way, the patient will learn and practice healthier ways of thinking and responding to anxiety-evoking situations to reduce OCD symptoms and improve quality of life.

- Assure the patient that you realize CBT is hard work. Review the advantages and disadvantages to this approach.
- Use the analogy of the therapist as a *coach*: you will work collaboratively with the patient to help him or her learn and practice a set of skills. You will never *force* him or her to do ERP techniques.
- Ensure that the patient understands that how much benefit a person gets from CBT is related to how much effort they put into doing the treatment.
- Recommend a trial of 16 sessions of CBT and answer any questions from the patient (and family members).

4

Treatment

4.1 Methods of Treatment

The "nuts and bolts" of conducting CBT

This chapter presents the nuts and bolts of how to plan and implement CBT for OCD. Table 10 shows the optimal schedule for what is to be accomplished in each treatment session. In our clinic, treatment might be delivered once-weekly, twice-weekly, or even daily depending on symptom severity and access issues (e.g., patients traveling from out of town often receive five daily sessions for 3 consecutive weeks). Research on methods to enhance extinction learning suggests that expanding spaced treatment sessions can optimize long-term symptom reduction (Craske, Treanor, Conway, Zbozinek, & Vervliet, 2014). For instance, you could begin with a few twice-weekly sessions, then several once-weekly sessions, then every other week, every third week, and

---

Table 10
Suggested Session Structure in Psychological Treatment for OCD

Session 1
- – Begin functional assessment of OCD symptoms
- – Introduce self-monitoring
- – Begin psychoeducation

Session 2
- – Continue functional assessment
- – Psychoeducation
- – Cognitive therapy
- – Begin planning for exposure

Session 3
- – Psychoeducation
- – Cognitive therapy
- – Finalize and agree on the exposure treatment plan

Sessions 4–14
- – Exposure
- – Response prevention
- – Cognitive therapy

Sessions 15 and 16
- – Final exposures
- – Relapse prevention
- – End response prevention
- – Assess outcome
- – Arrange for follow-up care (as necessary)

so on. However, in the interest of flexibility, the focus of this chapter is on mastery of the particular treatment *strategies* rather than on promoting a strict session-by-session agenda.

4.1.1 Functional Assessment

Functional assessment is the collection of highly detailed patient-specific information about obsessional triggers and the cognitive and behavioral responses to these stimuli, including a complete description of all compulsive rituals (behavioral and mental). The cognitive-behavioral model dictates what information is collected and how it is organized to form an individualized conceptualization of the problem and treatment plan. The Functional Assessment of OCD Symptoms form (see Appendix 1) is used to document this information. Depending on the complexity of the patient's symptoms, this assessment might last from 1 to 3 hr. Begin by providing a rationale for the detailed functional assessment that incorporates the following points:

> **Functional assessment – the collecting of detailed, patient-specific information**

- CBT involves learning skills to weaken OCD symptoms.
- To tailor the program to the patient's specific obsessions and rituals, you must have a very thorough understanding of these symptoms.
- Treatment will therefore begin by generating a list of all of the situations, thoughts, and other stimuli that evoke anxiety and urges to do rituals.

Assessing Obsessional Stimuli

Generate a comprehensive list of external triggers and internal stimuli (thoughts) that evoke obsessional fear. These stimuli might later be used in exposure exercises.

External Triggers

Identify all objects, situations, places, etc. that evoke obsessional fear and urges to ritualize. Examples include bathrooms, knives, doing paperwork, churches, the number "13," leaving the house, driving in certain places, reading about serial killers, and so on. Examples of questions to elicit this information include:

- What kinds of situations make you feel anxious?
- What situations make you feel uncertain about something that could go wrong?
- What triggers you to want to do rituals?
- What do you avoid because it triggers obsessions, anxiety, disgust, or rituals?

Obsessional Thoughts

In OCD, anxiety is also evoked by recurring ideas, images, doubts, and impulses that the patient finds upsetting, immoral, repulsive, or otherwise unacceptable. Examples include thoughts of germs and contamination, impulses to desecrate the church, unwanted images of genitalia, ideas concerning loved ones being injured, doubts about making mistakes, uncertainty about things that are difficult to know for sure (e.g., "am I going to heaven or hell

**Identify fears
of disastrous
consequences that
are immediate,
long-term, and
"unknowable"**

when I die?") and impulses to harm innocent people or loved ones. Examples of questions to elicit this information include:

- What unwanted intrusive thoughts do you have that trigger anxiety?
- What thoughts do you try to avoid, resist, or dismiss?

Assessing Cognitive Features

Obtain information about the following parameters of the cognitive basis of the patient's fear. This helps in developing effective exposure interventions to test out patients' predictions.

Fairly Immediate Feared Consequences

Patients may articulate fears that something terrible will happen if they are exposed to their obsessional stimuli or if they fail to perform certain rituals. For example, they would be responsible for injury to a loved one, become ill (if they do not wash), snap and commit a violent act, experience bad luck from confronting the number "13," or make serious or costly mistakes (e.g., with paperwork). Examples of questions to elicit such feared consequences include:

- What do you most fear from being exposed to [obsessional trigger]?
- What do you think might happen if you didn't do your _____ rituals?

Long-Term or "Unknowable" Feared Outcomes

Many people with OCD have feared consequences that might not materialize for a long time (e.g., many years). Examples include developing cancer someday, gradually evolving into a child molester, and being arrested by the police at some point for causing an automobile accident. Sometimes, the feared consequences are simply impossible to verify, such as "am I going to hell?", "am I disgusted enough when thinking about child abuse?", "am I faithful enough?", and "am I experiencing 'inappropriate' sexual arousal?" These types of feared consequences are driven by an intolerance of uncertainty, and questions to elicit them include:

- What is the worst thing you imagine might happen as a result of this situation (or obsessional thought) down the line?
- What terrible things that could happen to you later on do your rituals help to prevent?
- If you don't do your rituals correctly, what do you worry about most in the future?

Misinterpretations of Obsessional Thoughts

**Identify the ways in
which the patient
misinterprets
obsessional thoughts**

Identify mistaken beliefs about the presence and meaning of intrusive obsessional thoughts and images. For example, "Thinking about stabbing my wife could lead me to actually stab her," "God will punish me for thinking immoral thoughts," "I'm a pervert if I have unwanted thoughts about sex," and "Anyone who thinks violent thoughts must be a violent person." Examples of questions to elicit this information include:

- What do you think it means that you have this thought?
- What are you afraid might happen if you just let yourself have this thought?
- Why do you try to avoid or dismiss these thoughts?

Fears of Experiencing Long-Term Anxiety, Uncertainty, and Incompleteness

Some patients fear that anxiety (and arousal-related bodily sensations) will persist indefinitely, spiral "out of control," or cause other catastrophic consequences (e.g., physical harm) if allowed to continue without rituals or avoidance. This is often based on the belief that anxiety is intolerable or even harmful. In the same vein, patients sometimes describe the fear that uncertainty and doubt associated with an obsession (e.g., fears of "snapping" and committing murder) will continue indefinitely and become unbearable. Finally, patients with ordering and arranging compulsions often describe a sense of imperfection or incompleteness (also known as "not-just-right experiences") that they fear will persist or become intolerable if allowed to continue without performing rituals. Questions to help elicit these types of fears include:

- Do you worry that you will become anxious and that the anxiety will never go away?
- What might happen to you if you remained uncertain about this obsession?
- Do you worry that feelings of imperfection or incompleteness will stay with you forever?

Because these types of fears are not always readily apparent to the patient, some have difficulty articulating them. These individuals might require prompting to be able to describe such concerns (e.g., "Some people with OCD have the fear that if they don't ritualize, their anxiety will go on endlessly and become unbearable. Do you worry about this?").

Some patients do not articulate specific feared consequences, but instead worry that anxiety and uncertainty will persist

Assessing Anxiety-Reduction Behaviors

It is important to know about all of the patient's responses to obsessional fear (i.e., neutralizing, safety-seeking rituals, etc.) that serve to reduce or control unacceptable thoughts and anxiety. Such behaviors maintain OCD and will interfere with treatment if unassessed and not targeted in response prevention. In addition, the mere *availability* of safety cues and the *possibility* of performing anxiety-reducing behaviors should be taken into account; such as a patient reminding herself that she could always use the hand sanitizer stored in her car if anxiety became "too intense."

Determine the patient's maladaptive response to obsessional fear

Passive Avoidance

Most patients avoid situations and objects associated with obsessions in order to prevent feared disasters. Examples include avoidance of certain people (e.g., cancer patients), objects (e.g., knives), places (e.g., public washrooms), situations (e.g., using pesticides, bathing one's infant), and certain words (e.g., "devil"). Pay particular attention to subtle avoidance habits such as staying away from the most used surface or refraining from listening to music while driving. Ascertain the cognitive basis for avoidance (e.g., "if I touch the most used surface of the table, I will be more likely to get sick" or "if I listen to music, I might not realize it if I hit a pedestrian"). Examples of questions to elicit this information include:

- What situations do you avoid because of obsessional fear?
- Can you ever confront this situation?
- How does avoiding _____ make you feel more comfortable?

Overt Compulsive Rituals

List all ritualistic behaviors including cleaning, checking, repeating actions, arranging objects, and asking for reassurance. Attend to inconspicuous behaviors such as wiping, the use of special soaps, and excessive inspection (e.g., for signs of contamination). Determine the cognitive basis for rituals (i.e., the relationship between rituals and feared consequences). For example, checking to prevent fires and using a certain soap to target certain kinds of germs. Examples of questions to elicit this information include:

- What do you do when you can't avoid [insert situation]?
- Tell me about the strategies or rituals you use to reduce obsessional fear of [insert obsessional fear].
- How does doing this ritual reduce your discomfort?
- What might happen if you didn't engage in this ritual?

Mental Rituals and Covert Anxiety-Reduction Strategies

Inquire about mental rituals and other covert neutralizing strategies

Inquire about the use of mental rituals to neutralize unacceptable obsessional thoughts. Examples include thinking special "safe" thoughts, phrases, and images; repeating prayers in a set (or "perfect") way; mentally reviewing (over and over) one's actions to allay obsessional doubts; and habitual thought suppression and mental distraction. Ascertain the cognitive links between mental rituals and misinterpretations of particular obsessional thoughts. For example, repeating the phrase "God is good" to avoid punishment for having sacrilegious thoughts, and distracting oneself from violent thoughts to prevent acting violently. Examples of questions to elicit this information include:

- What kinds of mental strategies do you use to dismiss unwanted thoughts?
- How do you deal with your upsetting thoughts?
- What might happen if you didn't use these strategies?

Symptom Accommodation

For patients in relationships, and those living with close friends or family members, it is important to assess how others might be accommodating OCD symptoms. Such accommodation will need to be addressed during treatment. It might be helpful to include significant others (e.g., partner/spouse, parent, adult child) in the assessment session to collect this information. Some suggested questions for patients and their loved ones to help identify problematic relationship patterns concerning OCD symptoms include the following:

- What effects does OCD have on your relationship with _____ in terms of your daily life?
- Between you and _____, what patterns have developed because of OCD symptoms?
- How have you tried to cope with _____'s OCD symptoms?
- When _____ is experiencing obsessional fear or doing rituals, does it ever lead to anger or arguments? What happens in these situations?
- When _____ is having problems with OCD do you ever have a tendency to help him/her calm down from the anxiety, avoid situations, or assist with compulsive rituals to lower the anxiety?
- Tell me about how the two of you communicate about the OCD problem.

Assessing the Effects of OCD Symptoms on Quality of Life

OCD typically leads to disruption in one or more areas of functioning. Assess how it has interfered with the patient's life, noting even seemingly minor areas of interference. For example, the following questions could be asked:

- How does OCD get in the way of being successful at work/school?
- What kinds of problems do you have in your relationships because of OCD?
- How does OCD keep you from enjoying the things in life that you would like to enjoy?
- In what ways does OCD keep you from being as physically and emotionally healthy as you could be?

Clinical Pearl
The Play-By-Play Description

To gain additional insight into the patient's experience and how he or she copes with symptoms, you can ask for a "play-by-play" description of a few specific instances of obsessional fear, avoidance, and ritualistic behavior. This technique could also be used to focus the assessment on a particular symptom you are having difficulty understanding. It involves asking questions such as, "What was the situation in which obsessional distress was evoked?" and "What was the first sign of trouble?" Patients are asked to step through the situation and report their emotional and cognitive responses. What were they feeling and thinking? What happened next? How anxious did the patient become and what did they do to reduce this anxiety (rituals, avoidance)? How did the situation resolve itself and how did they feel afterwards? You can also point out the relationships between obsessions and increased distress, and between rituals or avoidance and anxiety reduction. Illustrating to the patient how these symptoms are related (as opposed to being bizarre or "out of control") can instill hope in the therapy program, as well as a sense of trust in your expertise.

> Ask the patient for a "play-by-play" description of OCD symptoms to illustrate a typical episode

4.1.2   Self-Monitoring

To aid the functional assessment, ask the patient to use the Self-Monitoring Form (see Appendix 2) to keep a real-time log of triggers that lead to rituals between sessions. Explain the form's importance and give instructions for completing it during the first session. Some patients fail to carefully and accurately self-monitor because they do not appreciate the task's relevance to treatment (many see it as "busy work"). To increase adherence, convey the following:

> Self-monitoring is an important (and often overlooked) component of CBT

- Self-monitoring helps both the therapist and the patient gain an accurate picture of the time spent engaged in, and situations that lead to, rituals.
- It helps the patient identify obsessions and rituals that he or she might not be aware of.
- Some patients use the fact that they have to record their rituals as motivation to resist them.
- Accurate reporting of rituals between now and the end of treatment will reveal how much progress is made in therapy.

With the patient's input, choose which rituals will be monitored (i.e., the most prominent ones). Then, give the following instructions:

- Rather than guess, use a watch to determine the exact amount of time spent ritualizing.
- To avoid forgetting important details, record each ritual *immediately*, rather than waiting until the end of the day (or worse, right before the next session).
- Write a *brief* summary of the situation or thought that evoked the ritual.

Ask the patient to self-monitor one or two recent rituals in the session to practice using the form. To further increase adherence, explain that the first item on the agenda for the next session will be to review the forms.

4.1.3   Psychoeducation

Psychoeducation helps socialize the patient to the cognitive-behavioral approach to OCD

The educational component of CBT helps lay the foundation for moving forward in treatment. You will teach the patient to think about OCD symptoms consistent with the cognitive-behavioral framework. You will also explain that ERP is used to foster fear tolerance (as opposed to emphasizing fear reduction) to maximize long-term learning and minimize relapse. The specific concepts to be conveyed are: (a) the symptoms and patterns involved in OCD are well-understood, (b) unwanted intrusive thoughts are normal, (c) dysfunctional interpretations of intrusive thoughts lead to obsessions, (d) avoidance and compulsive rituals maintain obsessions, and (e) treatment is based on this way of thinking about OCD. Presenting a coherent rationale is especially important since patients who do not see how ERP ultimately produces benefit cannot be expected to fully engage in these challenging techniques.

Understanding the Symptoms of OCD

Explaining the functional relationship between obsessions and rituals

Use the points below to begin with an explanation of OCD as involving three components. Include examples from the functional assessment to illustrate these points:

- A good way to think about OCD is that it has three parts.
- The first part is the *unwanted inner experiences*, such as unwelcome thoughts (obsessions) about _____, feelings of anxiety, fear, or disgust about _____, uncertainty and doubt about _____, a sense of incompleteness or imperfection, or other unpleasant sensations (e.g., racing heart). These experiences are mostly out of your control.
- The second part of OCD is your *attempts to get rid of the unwanted inner experiences*, such as by avoiding _____ and doing compulsive rituals, such as _____, that help you control, resist, or reduce the obsessional distress. These behaviors are mostly within your control, although it doesn't always seem that way.
- Although the behaviors in part 2 sometimes work temporarily, they trick you into using them more and more so that over time they develop into strong patterns. But avoidance and rituals are not good long-term solutions since the obsessions and anxiety always find a way to come back. So, you end up spending a great deal of time and energy on these counterproductive behaviors.

- The third part of OCD is the *disruption in your life*, such as how your problems with OCD interfere with your daily routine, work, leisure, social functioning, relationships, etc.
- It is important to keep in mind that it is mostly the strategies in part 2 that cause the disruption in your daily functioning, not the experiences in part 1.
- Given that avoidance and compulsions are easier to control than obsessions, and that the negative effects on quality of life are generally the product of (futile) attempts to avoid, resist, and control obsessional thoughts and other unpleasant inner experiences (rather than these experiences themselves), treatment for OCD will help you learn new ways to interact with obsessions, uncertainty, and anxiety, in order to lessen the need to engage in avoidance and rituals and improve your quality of life.

The next sections provide suggestions for how to present authoritative information about OCD and its treatment to help the patient become more acquainted with the cognitive-behavioral approach.

Normalizing Obsessional Thinking

Explain that unwanted, senseless, or bizarre intrusive (obsessional) thoughts, ideas, or images are part of all forms of OCD. Sometimes these thoughts are triggered by external stimuli (e.g., knives, toilets), whereas at other times they may be unprovoked (unwanted sexual images). Similarly, the experiences of anxiety (on an emotional and a physiological level) and uncertainty are ever-present in OCD. Research shows that unwanted thoughts (no matter how repugnant or upsetting) are normal experiences for over 90% of the population, and that these thoughts are usually not under our control (Rachman & Hodgson, 1980). People with OCD frequently misinterpret these kinds of thoughts as very significant and meaningful, whereas people without OCD simply consider them harmless "mental noise." As the therapist, it can be helpful to share examples of your own intrusive thoughts to demonstrate the normalcy of these experiences and to model acceptance of such "strange" occurrences. Most patients are surprised (and relieved) to find out that just about everyone has unwanted intrusive senseless.

Everyone has obsessional thoughts

If the patient wants to know *why* people have strange or unwanted thoughts in the first place, explain that the brain is highly developed and capable of enormous creativity. People can imagine all kinds of scenarios – pleasant and unpleasant. For example, many people daydream of winning the lottery or scoring the winning touchdown in the Superbowl. Just as our "thought generator" produces positive thoughts that are unlikely to come true, it can also produce unpleasant thoughts that are equally senseless.

Explain that anxiety is also a fundamental and critical part of being human. All humans (in fact, all animals) experience anxiety and fear as part of their "fight-or-flight" response when they perceive threat. The purpose of anxiety is to protect the animal from danger. In other words, we need anxiety – it is our friend. That said, anxiety can produce unpleasant physiological (e.g., racing heart, shortness of breath), emotional (e.g., racing thoughts, apprehension), and behavioral (e.g., restlessness, urge to escape) experiences. It is important to remember that despite their unpleasantness, all of these experiences serve a protective function (e.g., the heart races to pump blood to the body's muscles) to keep us safe from danger.

Dysfunctional beliefs and interpretations give rise to emotional distress

In OCD, however, the perceived threats that trigger the anxiety response are not actually dangerous – they usually pose no more than ordinary everyday risk (e.g., flushing the toilet, using the oven). Thus, obsessional anxiety can be viewed as a "false alarm." It is important for patients to think of anxiety and fear as fundamentally helpful and not inherently dangerous. For additional details on how to discuss this with patients, the reader is referred to Craske and Barlow's (2006) guide to the treatment of panic disorder.

Discuss with the patient that uncertainty is also an ever-present experience because it is impossible to be 100% certain of almost anything. People with OCD, however, have trouble tolerating even everyday levels of doubt and uncertainty (that most people accept and take for granted) when it comes to their obsessions. That is, where most people (without OCD) accept ordinary risks (e.g., using the oven), people with OCD perform unnecessary checking and reassurance-seeking behaviors (and other rituals) to try to obtain "iron clad" guarantees of safety (e.g., that they have not caused a fire). Overcoming OCD requires learning (and practicing) how to manage acceptable, everyday levels of risk and uncertainty.

Thus, underscore that the problem in OCD is not the occurrence of obsessional thoughts, anxiety, and uncertainty per se (remember that these are normal and universal experiences), but rather how the person *relates to* these experiences and perceives them as threatening. The aim of treatment is therefore not to eliminate obsessional thoughts, anxiety, and uncertainty, but rather to change one's relationship to these experiences. Once the patient sees these experiences as tolerable, rather than as threatening and insufferable, it won't matter when or how frequently they occur and there will be less need for rituals. Give the patient the Everyone Has Intrusive Thoughts handout (see Appendix 3) to be read after the session is over. The handout reviews this didactic information and includes a list of intrusive thoughts reported by people without OCD.

Normalizing intrusive thoughts is useful for individuals with any presentation of OCD, although the most straightforward application is for unacceptable aggressive, blasphemous, and sexual obsessions; and when intrusive doubts are present (e.g., persistent uncertainty about long-term or unknowable outcomes). For patients with contamination symptoms psychoeducation can be used to normalize feelings of disgust and contamination, and images of germs and uncertainty about illnesses. Senseless thoughts and ideas concerning the need for order, symmetry, balance, and exactness can also be normalized this way.

Patients may point out that although everyone has intrusive thoughts, their own intrusions are more frequent, more distressing, and more intense compared to those of nonsufferers. This may be true, and it is therefore important for patients to understand the role of thinking patterns (which they can learn to change) in causing normal intrusive thoughts to escalate into highly distressing and recurrent obsessions, as is discussed in the next section.

The Role of Dysfunctional Thoughts and Beliefs in OCD

The basis of CBT is the idea that emotional and behavioral responses are determined by one's *thoughts and beliefs* about situations, not by the situations themselves. It is helpful for patients to understand the process by which their own mistaken thoughts and beliefs lead to emotional responses such as anxiety. Strong emotions, in turn, exacerbate obsessional thinking.

For example, when someone with obsessions about germs drops an object on the floor and then picks it up, the following dysfunctional (i.e., exaggerated, mistaken, or rigid) thoughts and beliefs might be triggered: "Floors have lots of dangerous germs," "I am highly susceptible to illness," "I could get very sick," and "I can't handle not knowing for sure if I will get sick." These mistaken cognitions evoke distress and the urge to ritualize (i.e., washing and cleaning).

Clinical Vignette 1 illustrates the use of Socratic dialogue in which the therapist helps the patient understand how her thinking dictates her emotional and behavioral responses.

> **Helping the patient understand the relationship between thoughts and emotion**

Clinical Vignette 1
Illustration of the Cognitive Model With Non-OCD-Relevant Situation

Therapist: Suppose you and a friend plan to meet for dinner at 7:00 p.m. and it is now 7:30 p.m. and your friend hasn't shown up or even called to say that she'll be late. If you conclude that your friend decided that you are no fun to be with, how will you feel?

Patient: Sad or depressed.

Therapist: Right. How about if you believed your friend was being late on purpose just to jerk your chain?

Patient: Then I'd feel angry.

Therapist: Sure. How about if you thought that your friend had been in a terrible accident?

Patient: I'd be worried.

Therapist: Exactly. Do you see the importance of your thinking?

Patient: Yes. Depending on how I interpret the same situation, I could feel different emotions.

Therapist: That's right. The way you think about situations influences your emotional responses. So, you, not situations, have control over your emotions. This is called the "cognitive model of emotion.

After illustrating this model using a situation that is not emotionally charged, the next step is to apply it to an OCD-relevant situation, as in Vignette 2. The patient in the example had an excessive fear that she would catch the herpes virus from a particular coworker who once had a cold sore on her lip.

Clinical Vignette 2
Illustration of the Cognitive Model with OCD-Relevant Situation

Therapist: Now, let's see how the cognitive model might apply to OCD situations. You said that you become anxious and feel like washing your hands and changing your clothes whenever you are near this coworker. What kinds of thoughts would cause you to feel so anxious like you have to do these rituals?

Patient: I think that cold sores are easy to get from other people, so I assume I would probably get a cold sore if I came anywhere near her. On the other hand, if I wash and change, I won't get any cold sores.

Therapist: Do you see how your assumptions about the probability of you getting a cold sore lead to anxiety and the urge to do compulsive behaviors to prevent cold sores?

Patient: Yes, I see that.

Therapist: You said that other people don't wash themselves or change after interacting with this coworker. What must they be assuming about cold sores to keep them from feeling anxious or from having to do these rituals?

Patient: They probably don't think about it; or they just assume they won't get a cold sore unless there's intimate contact.

Therapist: Yes, that would make sense. Can you see that if you learned to think the same way, your coworker wouldn't seem so threatening anymore, and you wouldn't feel like you had to ritualize to stay safe?

Patient: I understand, but I can't just change my mind. I mean, I'm better safe than sorry, right!?

Therapist: That's what therapy is going to help you with. We're going to work together to help you learn how to get through these kinds of situations in ways that will be more effective for you. For now, though, it is important that you see how the cognitive model works. Your anxiety has a lot to do with thinking patterns.

In OCD the mistaken thoughts and beliefs are often about intrusive (obsessional) thoughts, rather than about situations. Applying the cognitive model with thoughts as triggers can be tricky since these stimuli, and the maladaptive thoughts and beliefs, are all mental events. Help the patient to distinguish between (a) intrusive obsessional thoughts and (b) thoughts and beliefs *about* these intrusions, as in the example in Vignette 3. The patient was devoutly religious, yet experienced unwanted sacrilegious thoughts such as "God is the devil's bitch" and "Jesus sucks." He interpreted these thoughts as meaning that despite a seemingly strong devotion to God, he was really a fraud (and devil worshipper). This provoked obsessional doubts about his salvation and constant prayer and reassurance-seeking rituals.

Clinical Vignette 3

Distinguishing Between Intrusive Obsessional Thoughts and Dysfunctional Beliefs

Therapist: You said that when these thoughts come to mind, you become uncertain about your faith and salvation, fear that you are a fraud, try to stop yourself from thinking these thoughts, pray for forgiveness, and seek reassurance that you are still a Christian. Can you see how you are interpreting your unwanted thoughts as very threatening?

Patient: Yes, I see that.

Therapist: How do you think those interpretations make you feel? What do they make you do?

Patient: They make me feel unsure and guilty, so I avoid churches and I am always praying.

Therapist: Right. So, the question is, Do these unwanted and senseless thoughts really mean you are a fraud? Do you really need to stop them completely in order to be a Christian? To put it another way, is it possible to practice your faith even without a 100% guarantee of salvation? Does anyone have a 100% ironclad guarantee about these kinds of things?

Patient: Well, if most people have unwanted thoughts, and if it's impossible to have a guarantee about things like faith and salvation, I guess you would say these thoughts and doubts are not really the problem. But that seems strange. I've worried about those thoughts and feelings for so long.

Therapist: That's because you have believed for a long time that those thoughts are very important and that you need to have a guarantee of your salvation. But actually, these thoughts and doubts are not even consistent with how you really feel about your religion. Everyone now and then has ideas that conflict with their personal beliefs and morals. Everyone experiences doubts at some point. In therapy, you will learn healthier ways to relate to these kinds of thoughts and doubts so that you are better able to practice your faith the way you want to and the way most other Christians do.

The Role of Avoidance, Rituals, and Other Anxiety-Reduction Strategies in Maintaining OCD

Help patients understand how their avoidance, rituals, and other attempts to reduce or control unpleasant inner experiences (e.g., thought suppression) contribute to the vicious cycle of OCD. This will provide a rationale for response prevention. Discuss the following points:

Explaining how safety-seeking behavior maintains obsessional fear

- Review how obsessions increase anxiety and compulsive rituals temporarily decrease anxiety.
- Aside from compulsive rituals, there are other strategies that people often use that have the same effects as rituals. These include avoidance, subtle (mini) rituals, seeking reassurance, and thought suppression attempts.
- Avoidance and rituals might seem strange, bizarre, or "uncontrollable." Help the patient view them as purposeful and deliberate anxiety-reduction strategies. Give an example of how rituals are used to neutralize obsessional anxiety or provide reassurance. Make sure the functional relationship between obsessions and compulsions is understood.
- Rituals would be adaptive responses if there were actual danger present. But, obsessional fear is based on mistaken thoughts and beliefs. So, these responses are unnecessary and counterproductive.
- Avoidance prevents patients from learning that their feared situations are not especially dangerous, and that the anxiety and uncertainty associated with situations and obsessional thoughts is manageable.
- When obsessional stimuli cannot be avoided, the next best solution seems like *escaping* from the feared situation and relieving the anxiety and uncertainty as quickly as possible in any way that seems to work (provide examples of how the patient's rituals are used to escape from obsessional fear). But this is a trap because the fact that these escape strategies sometimes reduce distress makes them develop into compulsive rituals that are difficult to stop.
- In summary, strategies used to avoid, control, or escape from obsessional thoughts, anxiety, and uncertainty often seem helpful in the

moment, but backfire in the long run since the obsessions and anxiety always return.
- Treatment will weaken these patterns by creating opportunities for the patient to learn that he or she can manage unpleasant obsessional experiences and situations without avoiding, ritualizing, or using other control strategies.

Clinical Pearl
Integrating Psychoeducation Into the Functional Assessment

A useful way to think about the initial sessions of CBT is as an exchange of information between patient and therapist. On the one hand, the patient is an "expert" on his or her particular OCD symptoms and must help the therapist understand the nuances of these symptoms in order that an individual treatment plan can be developed. On the other hand, the therapist is an expert in conceptualizing OCD symptoms and must teach the patient to understand his or her symptoms in a way that best fosters benefit from the treatment procedures.

In our clinic, we explain this situation to patients at the very beginning of the functional assessment phase. We weave the psychoeducational component into this assessment by capitalizing on any opportunities to help the patient understand the functional aspects of his or her symptoms. For example, when assessing obsessional thoughts, if a patient describes his or her intrusive thoughts as "strange" or "abnormal," or insinuates that he or she is the only person with such thoughts, we begin educating him or her immediately about the normalcy of unwanted thoughts. This technique helps socialize the patient to the cognitive-behavioral model of OCD, which is critical for a positive treatment response.

Presenting the Rationale for CBT and Explaining the Process

Presenting the rationale for using the specific CBT techniques to reduce OCD

Once the patient has a grasp of the cognitive-behavioral model, present a rationale for CBT by discussing the following points:
- The treatment techniques, *exposure* and *response prevention*, are designed to teach the patient that (a) obsessional thoughts, anxiety, and uncertainty – although unpleasant – are tolerable, and (b) the use of rituals and other anxiety-reduction strategies, which interfere with quality of life, are unnecessary. You *could* merely discuss these issues with the patient (i.e., cognitive therapy), but ERP provides real life experiential evidence, which is more convincing than just talking.
- Exposure involves confronting situations and thoughts that evoke obsessional anxiety and doubt. Response prevention involves refraining from doing anything to avoid, reduce, or control these internal experiences.
- Use information from the functional assessment to give examples of specific exposure and response preventions exercises that might be prescribed for the patient.

How to explain the concepts of *habituation* and *anxiety tolerance*

- One basic idea of exposure therapy is that repeatedly confronting situations and thoughts that evoke obsessional anxiety and uncertainty helps the patient learn that the anxiety and uncertainty often subside over time ("habituation").
- However, the most important point of exposure is that it teaches patients that the anxiety and uncertainty are tolerable and manageable regardless of whether these feelings subside or how long they take to subside.

Thus, *habituation is not required for exposure to be successful.*
- Since the patient has usually avoided or escaped from the obsessional distress by doing rituals, he or she has not had the opportunity to consistently practice tolerating these experiences. ERP will provide this opportunity.

Next, discuss what is likely to happen during exposure as follows:
- The patient should expect to feel anxious, especially when starting to confront the feared situation. But if he or she remains exposed without trying to control these feelings, one of two things will happen: The feelings will either begin to subside on their own, or they will remain present and the patient will discover that he or she can tolerate these feelings, even if they seem unpleasant.
- This learning only occurs if the exposure exercise is carefully designed and if the patient remains exposed without performing rituals and then repeats these exercises in different situations (e.g., theapist's office, home, in public).
- Two kinds of exposure are typically used in the treatment of OCD: *Situational* or *in vivo exposure* means facing the actual feared situations. *Imaginal exposure* means facing fears and doubts in imagination.
- ERP is likely to be very helpful, but it is hard work and must be done correctly in order to get good results.

Next, discuss how you will work with the patient to tailor the treatment program to his or her needs.
- The patient will help the therapist make a "to do" list of exposure stimuli that will include moderately anxiety-provoking situations up to those that are more difficult.
- Importantly, the exposure stimuli do not need to be confronted in any particular order. They might be completed hierarchically (i.e., beginning with easier stimuli and working up), or according to the patient's priorities, or based on how much they would improve quality of life.
- Although exposure exercises will usually be planned ahead of time as to avoid surprises, one possible "plan" is to randomly select exposures to maximize variability (to be discussed further in Section 4.1.6).
- The therapist will provide support and coaching during each exposure task in the session, and the patient will be asked to practice exposures independently between sessions.
- Sometimes, treatment instructions might seem especially risky, or involve doing (or thinking about) things that most people wouldn't ordinarily do (or think about) on purpose. The patient must understand that the purpose of ERP is not just to practice doing what *most people* do. These tasks are designed to foster tolerance of obsessional thoughts, anxiety, and uncertainty in order to weaken OCD symptoms and improve the patient's quality of life.

The patient should understand that treatment is tailored to his or her specific OCD symptoms

The relationship between patient and therapist in CBT is analogous to that between a student and a teacher, or between a ballplayer and a coach. In Vignette 4 the therapist explains his role as similar to that of a music teacher.

The therapist is essentially the patient's "coach" for overcoming OCD

Clinical Vignette 4
Describing the Patient/Therapist Relationship

Therapist: The best way to think of me is as your coach. Let's say you wanted to learn to play a musical instrument like the drums. You would go to a drum teacher who would give you instructions and then watch you play to look for things that you need to work on. The teacher would then help you improve your technique and tell you to practice hard between lessons. Now, if you didn't practice the new techniques, or if you practiced them in a different way from how the teacher taught you, you would not develop the skills needed to be a good drummer. Also, the teacher would not force you to practice – you would decide whether or not to practice. If you didn't practice, the teacher might encourage you to practice more, but eventually he or she might stop the lessons if it was clear that you weren't practicing enough.

Treatment for OCD goes the same way. I know how to create exercises that are designed especially for you to overcome OCD. If you practice these exercises the way that I show you, chances are you will see improvement. But, if you decide not to practice them as much as you should, or if you decide to change the exercises around, chances are you will not improve as much as you would like. I have a great deal of confidence in this treatment. But, I cannot force you to do the exercises – this is your therapy and the decision has to come from you. What I will do is help you see that although unpleasant, your feared situations, obsessional thoughts, and anxiety are tolerable – you can get through them; therefore, it is in your best interest to approach, rather than avoid them. We are on the same team against OCD. If you do the hard work in therapy, you will find that my coaching and support is very helpful.

4.1.4   Using Cognitive Therapy Techniques

Using cognitive therapy techniques

Cognitive therapy techniques for OCD teach patients to evaluate and modify maladaptive thinking patterns that give rise to obsessional fear and compulsive urges. This approach can help facilitate assessment, prevent premature discontinuation, and maximize adherence with ERP (Kozak & Coles, 2005), but we do not suggest using cognitive therapy techniques completely on their own (i.e., without exposure). Rather, we use these strategies informally throughout treatment in the context of ERP, often to reinforce what patients learn during exposure exercises. The primary style within cognitive therapy is *Socratic dialogue* in which the therapist promotes the patient's learning by asking questions and making comments to facilitate her or his independent, reflective, and critical thinking. Clinical Vignette 5 illustrates this type of dialogue, which is distinguished from didactic (i.e., lecture style) presentation of information. Ways of integrating cognitive therapy when OCD-related dysfunctional beliefs are present are discussed below.

Clinical Vignette 5

Example of Socratic Dialogue

Therapist: So, you are afraid to use the toilet where you work?

Patient: Yes. It seems like there are lots of germs in the staff bathroom because many people use that toilet. It's not safe and I am not doing exposure to touching it!

Therapist: What do you think would happen if you used the toilet?

Patient: I would catch a disease from the toilet seat.

Therapist: What kind of disease; and what would happen if you caught it?

Patient: I never thought about that exactly. I guess I would get so sick that I wouldn't be able to work.

Therapist: How about the other people at work? How do they feel about that particular toilet? Do they avoid it too?

Patient: No. I've seen most of them go into that bathroom.

Therapist: Hmm. So, your coworkers must get sick a lot.

Patient: [thinks]... Well, not really. Everyone is pretty healthy.

Therapist: Huh. So, what do you think it means if other people who use that bathroom stay healthy?

Patient: Maybe it's not as dangerous as I think. I never thought about it that way before. But, doesn't it make sense to avoid it just to be on the safe side?

Therapist: Well, I agree with you that the toilet is probably not as dangerous as you think, but what are the pros and cons of always trying to be on the "safe side" in a situation like this one? How has that interfered with your quality of life? What if you could learn to be more comfortable with this kind of uncertainty the way that your coworkers are?

Intolerance of Uncertainty

As we have discussed, one function of avoidance and compulsive rituals is to attain certainty about obsessional fears. It is as if patients believe they cannot handle the absence of complete reassurance (by contrast, nonsufferers take acceptable levels of uncertainty for granted on a daily basis). Put another way, people without OCD have the adaptive ability to *feel* certain about many things despite the fact that absolute certainty is more or less an illusion. You can use the demonstration in Clinical Vignette 6 to illustrate this problem:

> Help the patient understand how intolerance of uncertainty contributes to OCD

Clinical Vignette 6

Challenging Intolerance of Uncertainty About Non-OCD-Related Topics

Therapist: Think about your mother [who is not in the room]. Is she alive right now?

Patient: Of course. Why do you ask?

Therapist: I'm interested in how you know she's alive for sure?

Patient: When I was in the waiting room I talked with her on my cell phone.

Therapist: But that was 20 minutes ago. Isn't it possible that something terrible could have happened since then?

Patient: I guess so... So, maybe I don't know for certain that she's alive. But, I would bet that she's OK.

Point out that it is impossible to be 100% certain in most situations. Medical emergencies, after all, *can* occur at any time. Yet, in the vignette, the patient based her judgment on a *probability* as opposed to a *guarantee*. Next, discuss other reasonable "risks" that the patent takes on a regular basis (e.g., driving to and from the therapy session) to demonstrate that the patient knows how to properly manage everyday levels of uncertainty. To reduce OCD symptoms, however, he or she must be willing to practice living with uncertainty about obsessional fears as well.

Intolerance of uncertainty underlies obsessional fears of events that might occur in the *distant future* or are "unknowable" (e.g., cancer from long-term exposure to pesticides, going to Hell, becoming a pedophile). Patients often argue that they "cannot take the chance" of the feared event coming true. Here, you can point out that they would benefit by developing an alternative, less threatening, interpretation of the experience of uncertainty (that could subsequently be tested out using exposure techniques). This is illustrated in Clinical Vignette 7 with a patient whose obsessional fears concerned the possibility of developing schizophrenia:

Clinical Vignette 7
Managing Fears of Future Uncertain OCD-Related Events

Therapist: How have you been reacting to your doubts about developing schizophrenia?
Patient: Like I can't take the chance that I might go crazy.
Therapist: Right; and where does that lead you?
Patient: I get worried so I ask everyone for reassurance.
Therapist: Right. If you apply the same strategy that you say you used when I asked you about your mother, what could you tell yourself about those doubts that would help reduce OCD?
Patient: That the thoughts probably do not mean I am developing schizophrenia.
Therapist: That's right; they're probably just "mental noise" even though we don't have a guarantee. And although you can't really be 100% sure, you would probably be better off accepting some uncertainty and seeing this uncertainty as manageable. I bet you could learn to do this even though it might seem frightening. Do you think it would be worth testing out whether you could tolerate reasonable uncertainty about developing this disorder?

Significance of Thoughts (Thought–Action Fusion)

The belief that merely *thinking* blasphemous, aggressive, or sexual thoughts is equivalent to "immoral" behavior indicates the need for additional discussion regarding the normalcy of intrusive upsetting thoughts. Ask the patient what she or he thinks of the fact that even virtuous, ethical, and kind people sometimes have similar unwanted thoughts (e.g., about unpleasant or taboo topics). If a double standard is present, point this out and discuss alternative explanations. It might also be helpful to point out that it's impossible to truly know the moral nature of particular thoughts, and that trying to "pin this down" is akin to trying to obtain certainty about matters that cannot be known (i.e., it is a mental ritual).

If the patient believes that unwanted thoughts will cause or lead to the corresponding event, explore his or her ideas regarding the mechanism by which this could occur (e.g., "How do you think your thoughts of stabbing your baby will lead you to commit this action?" "How will thinking about your sister having a car accident make it happen?"). Inconsistencies with reasoning can then be explored through Socratic questioning to encourage the patient to rethink such assumptions (e.g., "If thoughts lead to actions, how are people able to maintain control of themselves when they get angry?" "Can you recall a time when you thought of something and it didn't happen?"). Exposure techniques, as described later in this chapter, can also be used to teach the patient that such reasoning is faulty.

If the patient is concerned that such obsessions imply he or she is a dangerous or immoral person, the discussion can focus on the "kinds" of people who would and would not be upset by violent, blasphemous, or sexual thoughts. Unlike the patient, someone intent on committing violence would not worry if they had thoughts about such behavior. A "pervert," for example, would not be upset by sexual impulses. An atheist would not be concerned over sacrilegious images.

Some patients might be afraid that they are "not bothered enough" by their unacceptable obsessions, and use this as the basis for their fear. This, however, implies intolerance of uncertainty regarding "how bothered is one supposed to be?" and "how much distress is enough?" These are unanswerable questions best addressed by learning to accept such uncertainties.

Does the patient have a history of behavior or thoughts consistent with these obsessions? (probably not). Thus, you might also point out that although one's history can be telling, it is still not a guarantee; and the patient is better off learning to tolerate the acceptable degree of uncertainty associated with these fears. Moreover, you might challenge the patient to find even one person who has never had an "immoral" thought. But does this imply that everyone is immoral?

You can use the experiment described in Vignette 8 to further illustrate this point: Hand the patient a delicate object and ask him or her to *think intently about* throwing the object across the room. When he or she does not throw the object, discuss the various factors that contribute to performing actions (e.g., decision-making). Thoughts, by themselves, do not translate to impulsively engaging in behaviors. This and other similar exercises (e.g., going outside and "wishing" for car accidents, wishing for the therapist to break her leg, buying a lottery ticket and thinking of winning) demonstrate that just thinking something does not make it happen and that one can tolerate having unpleasant intrusive thoughts.

Clinical Vignette 8

Illustration of the Cognitive Model With Non-OCD-Relevant Situation

Therapist:	[Hands the patient a paper weight and says]: I want you to think about throwing this paper weight through the window of my office. Just let yourself think about it for a while.
Patient:	Are you sure?
Therapist:	Yes. In fact, why don't you cock your arm back as if you were about to throw it.
Patient:	[Skeptically] All right; it's your window! (holds his arm up to throw, but never actually throws the paper weight)

> Therapist: [After about a minute] So, what's going on? How come you haven't thrown the weight?
> Patient: Well, obviously, I don't want to break your window.
> Therapist: That's interesting; but you've been thinking about it, right?
> Patient: Yes. I see what you're getting at.
> Therapist: And what is that?
> Patient: I guess it takes more than just thinking about doing something to make me do it.
> Therapist: Yeah, that seems right. And what other factors might influence your behavior.
> Patient: Well, it's the wrong thing to do and you'd probably make me pay for it.
> Therapist: So you're saying that you can make these decisions for yourself and that thoughts by themselves don't just translate into acting on impulse. Do you see how this relates to your obsessional thoughts of stabbing people you love?

Need to Control Thoughts

The need to control thoughts follows from dysfunctional beliefs about the importance of thoughts

The need to control thoughts follows from beliefs about the overimportance of thoughts. However, if patients are unaware of how their attempts at thought control are destined to fail, they might believe that (a) thought control is possible, and (b) since they cannot control their thoughts, something must be terribly wrong with their mind or brain. One technique for demonstrating the futility of attempts to control unwanted thoughts is to engage the patient in the following experiment:

> Therapist: *Let's try an experiment. I'd like you to try **not** to think of a pink elephant for one minute. You can think of anything else in the world **except** for a pink elephant. OK? Go.*

Invariably, the patient will think of pink elephants and agree that it is nearly impossible to fully suppress such thoughts. Next, ask the patient to explain how this phenomenon applies to obsessional thoughts. Such a discussion should focus on how attempts to suppress obsessional thoughts lead to more obsessions, and more futile attempts to suppress. It is understandable that at a certain point the patient would come to believe there is something terribly wrong since they cannot suppress their thoughts. Of course, suppression attempts are unnecessary since obsessional thoughts are not dangerous in the first place.

Perfectionism and the "Just Right" Error

In discussing beliefs about perfection, help the patient recognize that such an "all-or-nothing" approach is futile since perfection is largely an illusion. Help him or her to identify instances (unrelated to OCD) in which perfection is not demanded and in which there is no associated distress (e.g., books in no particular order on a bookshelf). This means the patient knows how to manage imperfection, yet must learn to apply this where OCD is concerned.

Severe perfectionism can interfere with the completion of therapy assignments (e.g., "If I can't do it perfectly, there's no sense in doing it at all"). In such cases, instruct the patient to purposely complete such tasks *imperfectly* to test out whether feared outcomes (e.g., failure to benefit) really occur.

Clinical Pearl
Capitalizing on Opportunities to Maximize Cognitive Change

A few examples of how cognitive therapy strategies can be applied at various points in CBT appear below.

- During exposure exercises (described in Section 4.1.7), help the patient process his or her experience. Review evidence regarding his or her ability to tolerate anxiety and uncertainty that is gleaned by performing the exercise. Help the patient articulate more realistic beliefs about the experiences of obsessional thoughts, anxiety, and uncertainty.

- When a patient shows strong affect, ask him or her to identify thoughts and images leading to their emotional response *at that moment*. Using Socratic questioning, address dysfunctional beliefs and assumptions. Apply this to OCD as well as to unrelated issues that may arise (e.g., a romantic break-up)

- Point out and summarize changes in beliefs (e.g., "I can't take not knowing for sure") during and after the completion of exposure exercises. Once the patient is socialized to the cognitive-behavioral model, ask him or her to provide such summaries.

- If self-monitoring forms indicate continued ritualizing, help the patient identify dysfunctional cognitions. For example, "What were you saying to yourself when you saw the fire engine and decided to go home to check whether the appliances were unplugged?" and "What were the short- and long-term consequences of your ritualizing?"

4.1.5   Using Acceptance-Based Strategies

Acceptance and Commitment Therapy (ACT; Hayes, Strosahl, & Wilson, 2011) is a set of techniques that can be applied in the treatment of OCD to help patients foster a willingness to experience their obsessional thoughts, uncertainty, and anxiety (Twohig et al., 2010). In our clinic, we often use ACT strategies to facilitate treatment engagement, but as with cognitive therapy, we suggest that these techniques are best used in the context of ERP, rather than on their own. Specifically, we use ACT strategies informally throughout treatment to help patients understand exposure therapy as a means of learning to respond flexibly in the presence of obsessions, anxiety, and uncertainty. ACT is also used to link specific exposures to improvements in quality of life and pursing things in life which the patient values.

The ACT perspective on OCD is consistent with the model we present in Chapter 2. While an important goal of both ACT and ERP is to broaden the patient's engagement with feared stimuli and improve quality of life, ACT explicitly focuses on (a) fostering willingness to experience obsessional distress, (b) recognizing thoughts and feelings as neither right nor wrong (i.e., "cognitive defusion"), and (c) using treatment to move toward what one values in life. For more information about ACT, the reader is referred to Hayes et al. (2011). Most ACT-based techniques take the form of metaphors that are discussed in the context of OCD and its treatment, and are referred to throughout treatment to revisit the processes described below.

Fostering Willingness

Willingness, in this context, refers to being open to "experiencing your own experience" without trying to change, avoid, or escape it; and without trying to attein certainty about its explanation. The metaphors in this section can be used to help the patient understand the goal of treatment as developing a healthier (more peaceful) relationship to OCD-related inner experiences.

Two Scales

Explain to the patient that it is relatively easy to rate the intensity of distress from obsessions on a scale from 0 to 10, and that he or she knows lots of triggers that increase distress, and uses avoidance and rituals to try to keep this distress as low as possible. However, these distress-reduction strategies work only temporarily and are not successful in the long term (i.e., anxiety always comes back up). Obsessions and anxiety are usually very difficult to control. But, there is another, less noticeable scale that is more important to focus on because it is easier to control; this is the "willingness scale" which also goes from 0 to 10, and represents how open the patient is to experiencing obsessions, anxiety and doubts without trying to change or avoid them. Initially, the patient has this scale set very low as indicated by the compulsive use of avoidance and rituals to try to resist obsessional distress. The problem is that when willingness is low, obsessional distress will often be high because this sort of distress only gets worse when it is resisted. That is, "if you don't want it, you'll have it," meaning that if the patient is unwilling to have obsessions, then obsessions are something to obsess about. Ask the patient what he or she thinks would happen if the willingness scale was set on "high." If this were the case, obsessions, anxiety, and feelings of uncertainty would be free to move around, come and go, etc. In other words, the patient would be changing how he or she relates to thoughts and feelings for the better. He or she wouldn't have to use avoidance and rituals to fight them anymore. Exposure practices help the patient set the willingness scale higher and you can inquire about the patient's level of willingness during exposures.

Jerk at the Door

In this metaphor, the patient imagines herself as hosting a party. She has invited her entire neighborhood, but then realizes that someone she doesn't like ("the jerk") has shown up at her door. The jerk represents all of the situations, thoughts, and feelings associated with OCD, and the patient spends her time guarding the door and trying to keep the jerk from coming in and ruining her party. In doing so, however, she is missing out on all the fun of the party (which represents her life). Ask the patient if she could welcome the jerk into the party, and be willing to have him there, even though she doesn't care for him and doesn't like that he showed up. This could lead to discussions about being willing to have obsessional thoughts, anxiety, and feelings of uncertainty even though they are unpleasant. ERP will create opportunities to practice "letting the jerk into the party."

Tug-of-War With a Monster

Set a scene in which the patient is about to play tug-of-war with a very strong monster (which represents OCD-related inner experiences). The patient is on one side of a large cliff, and the monster is on the other. The loser of this match will fall over the cliff. Discuss with the patient what options he has: He could (a) pull the monster over the cliff (which is unlikely given how big and strong the monster is), or (b) be pulled over the cliff by the monster. But then point out that there is a third option: to drop the rope and disengage from the fight. In this case, the monster would still be there but the fight would be over. The goal of ERP is to practice dropping the rope and living life even though the monster (i.e., anxious feelings, negative thoughts) is still there on the other side of the cliff.

Defusing From Thoughts and Feelings

People with OCD often give their thoughts, feelings, and body sensations a great deal of power, such as when they view certain internal experiences as objectively "good" (e.g., calmness, control) or "bad" (e.g., obsessions, anxiety, uncertainty). The following metaphors can be used to help shift away from rigidly evaluating OCD-related internal experiences in this way (e.g., as "dangerous," "immoral," etc.), and learn to step back and simply observe these thoughts and feelings. Put another way, the aim is to see obsessions and anxiety for what they really are (streams of words, passing sensations), not what they say they are (facts or dangers). The patient gets to decide for him or herself how much weight to give to particular experiences.

> **Defusion: seeing obsessions for what they *really* are, not what they *say* they are**

Passengers on the Bus Metaphor

In this metaphor, the patient is driving a bus (which represents progress toward the things he or she values in life) with some unpleasant passengers aboard. These passengers (which represent OCD-related inner experiences) are scary looking and they are yelling nasty threats (e.g., about obsessions, feared consequences, etc.) and demanding that the driver take the bus in a certain direction. The driver (patient) has struck a deal with these passengers: as long as they hide at the back of the bus and stop yelling nasty and threatening things, the patient promises to drive the bus wherever these passengers wish. This situation, however, represents giving in to OCD and letting it control one's life. One seeming alternative is for the driver to stop the bus and try to kick the passengers off. But not only will this not work (since the passengers are very strong), the driver has to stop the bus and so is no longer moving in the direction he or she wants to go in life. Most patients (drivers) have tried this and failed at various points. The best solution, therefore, is to continue driving the bus in the valued direction and recognize that the worst thing these passengers can do is come up to the front of the bus, look scary, and yell nasty and threatening things. Although they look scary, the passengers can't force the driver to go places he or she doesn't choose to go.

Becoming the Chess Board

Begin this metaphor by describing a game of chess with its two opposing teams. Team A represents the patient's OCD-related inner experiences (anxiety, obsessions, fears, doubts, etc.), while Team B represents feelings of safety and being in control. The patient is asked which team he or she would prefer to help win the game. But the therapist can point out that the two opposing teams are actually both within the patient; thus as soon as the patient chooses a side, he or she is fighting against a part of him or herself and therefore cannot win the battle. The therapist can then ask how things would be different if the patient was the *chess board*, instead of one of the teams. If the patient is part of a team, fighting and winning the game is very important, but if he or she is the board, he or she is in contact with the pieces (noticing them and remaining aware of what they are doing), but the outcome of the game is not important anymore.

Moving Toward Values in Life
Improving patients' quality of life is an important outcome of ERP. The point of the following exercise is to help patients realize that the hard work of treatment is worthwhile.

Moving Through a Swamp Metaphor
Ask the patient to think of his or her OCD-related inner experiences, and the situations that trigger them, as a swamp with mud, thick vegetation, moving rivers, quicksand, foul smells, and even creepy animals. On the other side of the swamp is a better quality of life. The patient can avoid going into the swamp and getting dirty, but then he or she is not heading toward the things that are important to him or her. ERP means learning how to handle whatever comes up while moving forward through this swamp. Point out that the patient is getting dirty for a reason – they are not just wallowing in the swamp; the point of ERP is not just to make the patient feel uncomfortable, but to move closer to what they want to get out of life.

4.1.6   Planning for Exposure and Response Prevention

The aim of ERP for OCD is to extinguish the anxiety and fear associated with obsessional stimuli (i.e., learned threat associations). Exposure techniques are used to engineer learning experiences in which obsessional stimuli are confronted without the use of rituals (i.e., response prevention). When the expected feared outcomes of exposure do not materialize, or are more tolerable than expected, it leads to the development of new learning. The *exposure list* is a catalogue of obsessional stimuli – the feared situations, thoughts, and other threat cues that the patient will confront during exposure sessions. Therapists can help the patient rate the expected level of distress when confronting each item. Traditionally, items are ranked according to distress level and confronted in a gradual fashion (i.e., progressing up a hierarchy). Recent research suggests that a more varied approach to exposure (e.g., randomly choosing from different levels of fear) teaches patients that they can tolerate varying levels of anxiety, which maximizes long-term maintenance of gains (Craske et al., 2014).

Designing the exposure list

Choosing Items for the Exposure List

External Cues
Informed by the functional assessment, and with the patient's assistance, compose a list of between 10 and 20 situations and stimuli that evoke the patient's

obsessional fear. Record these situations on the Exposure List form (see Appendix 4). Suggestions for choosing suitable exposure items appear below. Examples of exposure lists appear in Chapter 5.

The guiding principle when deciding on exposure items is that these situations and stimuli closely match the patient's particular obsessional fears. Therefore, patients with contamination fears might confront items such as floors, elevator buttons, toilets, shoes, door handles, bodily wastes and secretions, pesticides, hospitals, "contaminated" people (e.g., shaking hands), etc. Items that serve as reminders of contaminants (e.g., roll of toilet paper) might also be incorporated if such stimuli are avoided. Exposure for patients with fears of mistakes or harm (negligence) might involve leaving the stove on and going outside, locking the door in a "careless" way, completing assignments hastily, driving past pedestrians, or thinking of insults before sending emails to important people (for someone afraid of sending insulting messages by mistake). Individuals with fears of bad luck might confront "unlucky" numbers (e.g., 13, 666) or words (e.g., "death"). Those with violent obsessions would confront items that trigger violent thoughts, such as knives and news stories about violence. Those with sexual or religious obsessions would confront items such as pornographic material and religious icons. Finally, for patients with concerns about symmetry and order, exposure would entail confronting the kinds of imperfection, disorder, imbalance, etc. that the person tries to avoid. Details for how to conduct exposure to these various stimuli are provided in Section 4.1.7

Choose exposure tasks that represent "ordinary levels of risk" within the confines of your (or an expert's) judgment. Situations or stimuli that evoke the patient's worst obsessional fears must be included on the exposure list in order for patients to maximally benefit from treatment. Failure to confront items that trigger high levels of anxiety prevents the full extinction of obsessional fear and reinforces the mistaken idea that such situations (and high levels of anxiety or fear) should be avoided because they really *are* too dangerous. This leaves patients vulnerable to the return of obsessional fear.

It is not essential that every possible fear cue appear on the exposure list. Items should be detailed enough to advise the patient and therapist of the nature of the exposure exercises (public bathrooms), yet leave open the option to vary the specific task(s) in accord with the patient's specific fears and in different contexts (e.g., bathrooms at the mall, restaurants, gas stations, etc.). This permits flexibility in developing exposures of varying degrees of difficulty as needed (some of which might not be contrived until the particular exposure is begun). Clinical Vignette 9 illustrates how to include the patient in selecting exposure items.

Clinical Vignette 9
Putting Together an Exposure List

Therapist: You said that you limit your driving because you are afraid of hitting pedestrians. So, it sounds like a good situation for you to practice for exposure would be driving through the mall parking lot on a weekend afternoon.

> Patient: Oh God, I couldn't do that! I'd be too afraid. Maybe I could do it on a weekday when there are fewer people around.
>
> Therapist: Well, as you know, the point of exposure is to practice taking risks where you feel afraid so you can learn that these situations are safer than you think and see that you can handle the anxious feelings better than you expected. So, suppose we begin with driving through the parking lot on a weekday and then come back on a weekend? We can also try this exposure during the nighttime to help you learn that it is reasonably safe at different times of the day; but avoiding the weekend scenario altogether would not be a good choice.
>
> Patient: I know, but it's hard for me to do.
>
> Therapist: That's why I'm OK with us starting where you would like to start. As long as we change up the exposure from there, it is likely to help you.

Internal Cues

Imaginal exposure provides a systematic way of repeating and prolonging confrontation with intrusive obsessional thoughts, images, and urges that evoke anxiety. Scenes to be imagined are chosen from the list of obsessional thoughts and ideas of feared consequences generated during the functional assessment. Brief descriptions of these scenes are entered onto the Exposure List form as well.

Imaginal exposure can be used in different ways, and either alone or in combination with exposure to external cues. Patients can imaginally confront anxiety-evoking intrusive thoughts, images, and urges such as distressing, graphic, vulgar, or sacrilegious images (e.g., descriptions of accidents involving loved ones) as well as thoughts of, and uncertainty regarding, the feared consequences of exposure without performing rituals. For example, a patient with fears of causing house fires by mistake might leave the iron plugged in (situational exposure) and, after leaving her home without checking, purposely imagine that she has caused a serious fire.

Targeting feared consequences that are in the distant future or are unknowable

Clinical Pearl
Targeting Feared Consequences With Exposure

The best exposures are those which allow the patient to test (and disconfirm) their fears of disastrous consequences (e.g., "I will hit people with the car"). However, in some instances feared consequences pertain to disasters either in the distant future (e.g., developing cancer in 10 years) or that are unknowable (e.g., going to hell) and are therefore not subject to immediate disconfirmation. In such cases, exposure tasks should be designed with the understanding that the aim is to learn to tolerate acceptable levels of risk and uncertainty. Specifically, the patient can confront the feared situation or image and then test their ability to manage the associated uncertainty. Because anxiety and uncertainty are common experiences for people (especially with OCD), it is important to help the patient disconfirm the expectation that he or she needs to perform rituals in order to deal with these feelings.

Rating Items on the Exposure List

The SUDS scale

Once an initial list of items is generated, ask the patient to assign a numerical rating of subjective units of distress (SUDS) for each item (i.e., "How anxious would you feel if you confronted _____?"). The SUDS scale includes every number from 0 (no distress) to 100 (maximal distress), although it can be introduced using the anchors shown below:

- 0 SUDS = no distress (like you are asleep)
- 25 SUDS = minimal distress
- 50 SUDS = moderate distress
- 75 SUDS = high distress
- 100 SUDS = maximum distress (e.g., being tied to the railroad tracks as the train is coming around the bend!)

Record the patient's SUDs rating for each item on the Exposure List form. Some considerations for using the exposure list to generate a treatment plan are as follows:
- One might begin with moderately distressing items (e.g., 40 SUDS) and work gradually up to those most distressing. A limitation of this approach is that it implicitly teaches patients that higher levels of anxiety are more threatening or more difficult to manage than are low levels. This is problematic because it reinforces the experience of anxiety as a fear stimulus.
- Another approach is to allow patients to select the order of exposures based on what items most interfere with functioning.
- A third option is to randomly choose exposure items from the list (e.g., picking out of a hat). This maximizes variability in provoked anxiety, which helps solidify learning.
- The most anxiety-provoking items must be confronted in order for patients to experience maximum treatment gains.
- All exposure exercises should be repeated in different contexts (e.g., locations, unaccompanied, time of day).
- Over the course of treatment, the patient should gradually take more of an active role in designing and implementing exposures.
- Items that were inadvertently omitted from the exposure list can always be added after discussion with the patient.
- Each item is first confronted under the therapist's supervision and then practiced between sessions.

The Response Prevention Plan

Although the term "response prevention" engenders images of physically restraining patients from performing rituals, the procedure is fully voluntary. Optimally, the patient completely abstains from all rituals and neutralizing behaviors beginning with the first exposure session. However, most patients require a gradual approach to stopping. Key considerations when planning for response prevention appear below.
- Revisit the educational materials presented in earlier sections and emphasize the importance of *choosing not to ritualize.*
- Define the limits of response prevention and do not require that patients take more than acceptable risks. For example, if "no checking mirrors while driving" is a rule, allow for an exception when going in reverse (e.g., one brief check).
- Do not violate cultural or hygienic norms. Patients with washing rituals, for example, should be allowed to shower and brush their teeth daily.

The response prevention plan

However, they should "reexpose" themselves to contaminants following a shower.

- Specify abstinence from "mini rituals" and subtle safety behaviors that might not initially be recognized (or reported) as OCD symptoms (e.g., reassurance-seeking).
- If relatives or friends are involved in the patient's rituals, encourage their help with response prevention.
- For patients who are initially unable to cease all rituals, consider a gradual approach in which instructions to stop rituals parallel exposure practices. For example, once a patient confronts "trash can germs" during exposure, he or she would be asked to refrain from washing after taking out the trash or throwing something away; but not necessarily after using the bathroom if exposure to bathrooms has not yet been practiced (although they should reexpose to trash cans after such a wash).
- In situations where the patient feels he or she cannot refrain from a ritual indefinitely, "response delay" can be used in which the ritual is put off for a given period of time (and the patient is challenged to see how long she can go before performing the ritual).
- Instruct patients to record violations of response prevention on Self-Monitoring Forms. Violations indicate trouble spots that require additional work.

Clinical Pearl
Enlisting a Designated Support Person

Some patients encounter difficulty conducting exposure and response prevention tasks independently (between sessions). It may be useful in such cases to designate a "support person" such as a close friend or relative who agrees to be available for the patient to assist with treatment (when called upon by the patient). The support person should meet with the therapist to receive instruction in how to help with treatment. The best support persons are those who are able to be empathic yet firm. Individuals who are over-involved in the patient's symptoms, or who are overly critical or harsh, should be avoided. The support person is to report any adherence problems to the therapist.

Ideas for implementing response prevention for common compulsive rituals

Some typical response prevention rules for common presentations of OCD are as follows:

Decontamination Rituals:

Patients are not to use water (i.e., no washing) or other cleaning agents (e.g., hand gels, wet wipes) on their body. Creams, make-up, bath powder, and deodorants are allowed as long as they are not used to reduce contamination fears. Water may be drunk or used when brushing teeth, but not to clean the face or hands (shaving should be done with an electric razor). One daily 10-min shower is permitted, but ritualistic washing of specific body parts is not allowed (unless medical conditions necessitate such cleansing). Following the 10-min shower, the patient is asked to recontaminate with items from earlier exposures.

Checking, Counting, Arranging, and Repeating Rituals:

The patient is not to engage in any repetitive behavior. For example, only *one* brief glance in the rearview mirror when driving, *one* quick check of the door when leaving the home, *one* rapid proof for errors when completing paperwork, etc. Checking and counting are not allowed for items normally not checked (e.g., appliances) or counted (e.g., steps). Counting and checking rituals may be foiled by counting incorrectly, checking incompletely, or noting to oneself that he or she is not 100% certain of the outcome of the check. Actions repeated because of the presence of "bad thoughts" (e.g., going back and forth through a doorway until blasphemous thoughts are successfully suppressed) are not to be repeated. Arranging items that appear imperfect is not allowed.

Reassurance-Seeking Rituals:

Compulsive reassurance-seeking from family members, "experts" (e.g., priests, doctors), or from the therapist, is not permitted. It is helpful to discuss with patients the difference between *assurance* (asking a question to gather new information) and *reassurance* (asking a question when the answer is already known in order to reduce anxiety). It can also be useful to educate other individuals (e.g., family, friends) from whom the patient habitually seeks reassurance about the need to refrain from answering these types of questions during treatment. Suggest that they respond in a supportive way or refer the patient back to you. For example, "It sounds like you're seeking reassurance. I'm sorry but I can't answer that question because I agreed to help you with treatment. What else could I do to help you manage your discomfort?"

Mental Rituals:

Patients are to refrain from mental strategies for canceling (neutralizing) or "putting right" unacceptable thoughts. Ritualized praying (i.e., used to deal with obsessional fear) is prohibited. Arranging response prevention for mental rituals requires a discussion with the patient. He or she might already have a method for blocking such rituals. If mental rituals cannot be easily stopped, you can suggest that the patient (a) think of an *upsetting* thought instead; or (b) perform the mental ritual incorrectly. For example, if the ritual is to mentally reassure oneself by reviewing events (e.g., to be sure one did not say racial slurs), the review should be purposely foiled (e.g., "I *might have* used a racial slur").

Agreeing on the Treatment Plan

Before exposure begins, the patient and therapist both agree to adhere to the treatment plan. Review the following points before moving on:

- Beginning with the next session, the patient will practice facing the situations and thoughts on the exposure list in session (with the therapist) and between therapy sessions (independently).
- The patient will also practice refraining from rituals as planned and let the therapist know if he or she is having problems with resisting the urges. Resisting rituals will teach the patient healthier ways to relate to obsessional fear.

The patient and therapist must agree on the treatment plan before ERP begins

- If an urge cannot be resisted, the ritual should be recorded on the self-monitoring form and the patient should reexpose him or herself to the situation or thought which evoked the ritual.
- Daily self-guided exposure tasks will be assigned for practice between sessions. These tasks may be practiced alone or with the supervision of a designated support person, but should be practiced in varied settings and contexts to be maximally effective.
- The patient should expect to feel anxious when first facing each new situation, and understand that although challenging in the beginning, things will get easier for them with repeated practice.
- The therapist will not force the patient into exposure tasks, but will *encourage* him or her to choose exposure instead of avoidance.
- The therapist will assume the role of a coach who provides instruction and support throughout treatment. This means encouraging the patient to face his or her fears and *work through* the distress, rather than making the distress go away for the patient.
- Treatment should not proceed until the patient agrees to this treatment plan.

4.1.7   Implementing Exposure and Response Prevention

Implementing exposure and response prevention

This section describes how to conduct exposure therapy for OCD. The basic format of each exposure session is outlined in Table 11. The primary aim of exposure is to confront the predetermined fear cue(s) without performing rituals. In some exposure sessions, anxiety levels will decline over time, while in others, this habituation may not occur. Because the goal is to learn anxiety tolerance, each exposure can continue until either the distress level (and compulsive urges) dissipates on its own, or the patient is able to manage the distress that is present. Accordingly, there is no rule about the duration of each exposure session.

Clinical Pearl
Goals for Early Exposure Sessions

To strengthen the patient's trust and participation in exposure therapy, it is important to appear hopeful and confident. Showing an understanding of the patient's OCD symptoms, being up front when discussing the treatment procedures, and taking seriously the patient's input also helps strengthen the patient's conviction in the treatment program.

During initial exposure sessions, help the patient develop good "work habits" for performing these tasks by attending to (and shaping) the patient's behavior. Many will have never tried this type of exercise before. Explain why exposure is to be done in ways that evoke distress. Be democratic (as opposed to autocratic) and show sensitivity to help the patient view you as an advocate, rather than a taskmaster.

Table 11
Components of Exposure Sessions

Procedure	Approximate time
• Checking in • Checking homework • Reviewing self-monitoring forms	15 min
• Conducting the exposure exercise	45–60 min
• Agreeing on homework practice	5 min
• Planning for the next session's exposure	10 min

Checking Homework and Reviewing Self-Monitoring Forms

Each exposure session begins with a general check-in and review of homework assignments. All forms are inspected and the patient provides a qualitative report of his or her work between sessions. Follow up on the assignments you gave the patient, and review self-monitoring forms to reinforce the importance of working hard between sessions. This will also help you determine whether all instructions have been followed correctly. Use praise to further reinforce successful completion (or sufficient effort toward completing) assigned tasks. Be sure to discuss what the patent has learned from completing each assignment. When assignments are not completed as instructed, troubleshoot and, if necessary, complete the homework in that day's session before moving on.

Reinforce the importance of homework by checking the patient's forms at the start of each session

Introducing the Exposure Task

Begin by describing the specifics of the planned exposure task, including how the feared stimulus will be confronted, and what kinds of anxiety-reduction behaviors (e.g., rituals) are to be resisted during and after the exercise. Then, help the patient identify feared consequences of performing the exposure task. Some patients will articulate short-term consequences that can easily be tested during exposure, such as whether thinking racial slurs will lead to blurting them out loud, or whether leaving an appliance plugged in while out of the house will result in a fire. Others will fear long-term or unknowable consequences, such as getting sick *in 10 years* or causing bad luck to a loved one not in the room. Such concerns, however, also have a short-term fear component – the immediate fear involves not knowing for sure whether the long-term consequences will occur (i.e., the fear/intolerance of uncertainty). Thus, exposure can be used to help the patient discover that such uncertainty is manageable (i.e., not threatening enough to warrant avoidance or rituals).

How to introduce the exposure task

Accordingly, when fears of long-term consequences are present, help the patient identify shorter-term feared consequences that can be tested within the exposure session, such as "I won't be able to handle the uncertainty for more than a few minutes," "The anxiety will be too much for me to take and I will have to do a ritual," and "I won't be able to tolerate feeling 'not just right' for very long." Exposures to the possibility of these feared outcomes will test the patient's beliefs about how long he or she can put up with distress without escaping by ritualizing. Ask the patient for an estimate of how long they expect to be able to continue the exposure and endure the anxiety and uncertainty without ritualizing.

To give the patient an idea of how the exercise is to proceed, review the Guidelines for Conducting Exposure handout (see Appendix 5) before beginning the first exposure. A brief description of the exercise, the feared consequences, and an initial SUDS rating should be entered on the Exposure Practice Form (see Appendix 6), which is used to keep track of progress during each exercise.

A typical introduction to an exposure task is as follows:

Therapist: *At the end of our last meeting, we agreed that the exposure task for today would be for you to practice writing words you've been avoiding, such as "sin" and "demon." By the end of today's session, I'd like you to be writing even the most distressing words like "hell" and "devil." So, you will practice writing these words over and over on this pad of paper. I also want you to allow yourself to think about any distressing thoughts that may come to mind, such as the blasphemous images you are bothered by. Your job is to practice not "canceling out" these thoughts, or using prayer or confession rituals to make you feel less distressed. Just let the thoughts "hang out" in your mind. I know this is going to produce anxiety for you, but doing this exposure will help teach you that you can allow those thoughts to be there without trying to control them. You might even see that your distress subsides when you don't try to fight the thoughts anymore. This exercise will also help you gain a sense of mastery over your fear. I will be keeping track of your anxiety level (SUDS) during the exposure by asking you to rate it every five minutes so you can see that you can handle these feelings better that you may think. So, have in mind a number between 1 and 100 to give me. Are you ready?*

Conducting Exposure Exercises

How to conduct exposure exercises for common OCD symptoms

The aim of each exposure is to provide opportunities for the patient to develop new nonthreat associations with feared stimuli (both external situations and feelings of anxiety and uncertainty themselves). In order to maximize this learning, conduct exposures so that they violate the patient's fear-based expectancies about obsessional stimuli as written on the Exposure Practice Form (e.g., "I will get sick within 3 days," "I won't be able to tolerate not knowing if God is upset with me for more than a few minutes"). In some instances, this will involve learning that feared stimuli are acceptably safe (i.e., the feared outcome is not as likely or as severe as was predicted). In others, it will involve learning that feelings of distress/fear/anxiety and uncertainty themselves are safe and manageable. Accordingly, exposure concludes when patients' expectations of the danger or intolerability of feared stimuli have been contradicted. Learning focuses on whether the expected negative outcome occurred, or was as "awful" as expected (i.e., whether it was "manageable"). In some cases this will require that exposures be prolonged and repeated more than once.

A suggested strategy for enhancing extinction learning is to combine multiple fear cues during exposure sessions. For example, if a patient's obsessional fear of harming loved ones is evoked by knives and by stories about serial killers, this patient might read stories about serial killers while handling knives in the presence of loved ones (note that these various exposures – being in the presence of loved ones, handling knives, and reading about killers – would first be conducted separately prior to being combined).

At regular intervals during the exposure, ask the patient to rate his or her anxiety level and urge to ritualize, and record these ratings on the Exposure Practice Form. Research suggests that asking patients to put their feelings into words and speak them out loud helps consolidate learning during exposure. We therefore encourage therapists to ask questions such as "How are you feeling now?" and "What are you telling yourself about doing this exposure?" and record answers (e.g., "I'm feeling very scared that I've caused an accident and I want to go back and check") on the Exposure Practice Form.

While it is important to maintain a general focus on the exposure task, the conversation may occasionally drift off topic. When this occurs naturally, you can point out that the patient is able to have a casual conversation even while confronting his or her fear and experiencing anxiety and uncertainty. This can also help to consolidate learning about one's ability to tolerate the experience. This is different from purposeful distraction from the exposure task, which is counter-indicated.

When the exposure is complete, help to further consolidate what has been learned by asking the patient to articulate what he or she learned during the experience. Did the fears come true? Were anxiety and uncertainty truly unbearable? What surprised the patient about doing the exposure? The answers to these types of questions can be discussed in the context of the patient's violated expectations about the difficulty of the exposure. Help the patient recognize that he or she can cope better than predicted with obsessional thoughts, anxiety, or uncertainty about feared consequences.

The next sections present detailed instructions for conducting situational and imaginal exposures for common presentations of OCD.

Contamination Fears

Begin by encouraging the patient to touch the feared contaminant. If necessary, during early exposures, you might model this by touching the stimulus yourself. The patient must *fully* confront the feared stimulus – briefly touching it with fingertips does not count. It is important for the patient to feel thoroughly contaminated and vulnerable to feared consequences.

Clinical Vignette 10 illustrates exposure to a "contaminated" towel from the patient's home bathroom. Note how the therapist structures the exposure to disconfirm the patient's expectations about how long she can manage touching the towel.

Clinical Vignette 10
Example of an Exposure Exercise With Contamination Fears

Therapist: How about if we start with you touching the towel with your whole hand.

Patient: [Hesitates] ...OK. [Holds on to the towel.] There.

Therapist: Good job. So, how do you feel right now?

Patient: I'm scared that I'm going to get very sick from touching this disgusting towel since it was near the toilet when it overflowed. I'm not sure how long I can stand doing this, though.
Therapist: You're doing great. It's OK to feel anxious – remember the "bring it on" attitude! Anxiety is the raw material of change. It's worth feeling anxious now so that you can learn how to handle feelings of contamination and anxiety in the future. You predicted that you could touch the towel for 5 minutes. Let's see if you can surprise yourself. What is your SUDS rating?
Patient: About 80 [therapist records this on the form].
Therapist: How strong is your urge to wash your hands?
Patient: Pretty strong. Like 85%.
Therapist: You're doing great. Keep holding on to the towel.

15 Minutes later...

Therapist: So, 15 minutes have now passed, and you're still holding the towel. What do you make of that?
Patient: I'm surprised I could do it, but it does seem to be getting easier.
Therapist: Good for you! How long do you think you could keep holding it now?
Patient: I think I could do it for the rest of the session. I'm pretty confident even though my SUDS is still at 65.

Amplifying refers to deliberately intensifying an exposure in order to address a particular aspect of avoidance and to further test the patients' expectations. For contamination exposures, this usually means contaminating items or body parts the patient tries to avoid tainting (e.g., purse, wallet, face, hair, mouth). As an example, the patient in Vignette 10 was instructed to put the towel in her lap and to touch it to her arms, legs, and face. This was repeated every 5–10 min varying areas of the body that were touched. For instance, she touched the towel to her purse (inside and out), hair, and jacket for longer than she thought she could.

Look for subtle avoidance and rituals such as wiping, opening doors with one's feet, and other curious maneuvers that most people don't do. Patients who appear to "space out" during exposure should be asked whether they are engaging in purposeful distraction or other strategies such as praying and analyzing the chances of getting sick. These rituals might be so habitual that they occur without the patient's awareness. Therefore, try to bring them to the patient's attention whenever they are observed.

The importance of matching the exposure situation to the patient's obsessional fear cannot be overstated. Patients fearful of "spreading" contamination to other people should practice shaking hands with "innocent" others. Those fearful of "floor germs" can conduct entire sessions seated on the floor (in a public bathroom, for example). For those concerned with bodily waste and fluids, we supervise direct confrontation with such substances (or situations in which the substances *might* be present). Examples include, putting a drop of urine on the hand, deliberately stepping in dog poop and wiping it off with a tissue, and handling dirty towels found in the gym locker room (to confront a fear of sweat).

Obsessional Doubts of Harm and Negligence

Carrying out exposure for harming symptoms can be more complicated than for contamination symptoms. This is because harming obsessions and checking rituals are usually triggered by circumstances in which the patient perceives a risk of being responsible for causing (or failing to prevent) harm, injury, or damage. So, you should be cautious since the patient can transfer responsibility for any negative consequences onto the therapist.

To further complicate matters, many situational exposures for harming symptoms would be compromised if they are prolonged or repeated during the same session. For example, plugging in the iron or turning on the stove can only be done once during a single session because repeating these exercises is inherently a check that no fire has started. Therefore, take precautions to ensure that no de facto reassurance seeking occurs that would invalidate the exposure. For example, have the patient perform these actions once, and then promptly leave the premises without checking. The exposure can be prolonged using imaginal exposure to uncertainty about whether the feared consequences will or have occurred (e.g., the house burning down). In these types of exposure, the patient will test beliefs about his or her ability to manage uncertainty about these feared consequences for certain lengths of time ("I couldn't think about a fire and go without checking the house for more than an hour").

Some examples of exposure assignments for patients with harming symptoms and checking rituals are as follows: A patient who fears hitting pedestrians can perform driving exposures without checking the roadside or mirror. Someone fearful of causing a fire or a burglary can practice carelessly turning off lights and appliances, or closing and locking doors, without checking. A patient with fears of stabbing others can use knives and pins around other people. Someone with fears of cursing or insulting others can practice writing and saying curse words.

When the feared act of commission or omission presents a very low risk of harm, exposure can involve deliberately carrying out such behaviors. A few examples are as follows: a patient who fears that failing to warn others of glass on the floor will result in someone being injured can purposely place pieces of glass on the floor of a crowded area, refrain from warning people, and then practice imaginal exposure to the possibility that he or she caused injury. Someone fearful of starting a fire can intentionally leave appliances (even the stove) on and unattended for an acceptable period of time. A patient who fears miswriting an address on an envelope can purposely misspell the addressee's name, street, or city. A person who fears performing imperfectly could purposefully commit minor "imperfections" as exposure tasks. Someone afraid of numbers such as 13 or 666 can deliberately write these numbers on their hand or on pictures of people they would not want to "curse."

As mentioned previously, imaginal exposure should be integrated with situational exposure when patients report feared consequences of not checking. For example, a patient with obsessional fears of leaving confidential information in plain view at work first completed a situational exposure involving handling confidential files, putting them away while distracted with music (he feared this would make him more likely to make such a mistake), and leaving for home without checking. Next, as an imaginal exposure, he confronted obsessional thoughts of mistakenly leaving files in plain sight, being caught

Exposure for harming, injury, and mistake obsessions can be complex

and fired, and then being sued. The therapist introduced the imaginal exposure as in Clinical Vignette 11:

Clinical Vignette 11
Introducing an Imaginal Exposure

Therapist: You said that when obsessional doubts of violating confidentiality come to mind, you often return to work to make sure you haven't left any confidential materials out on your desk. To help you learn healthier ways of responding to these obsessional doubts and urges to check, you can practice thinking the obsessional doubts, but instead of checking, allow the doubt and uncertainty to remain in your mind. Concentrate on the distressing thoughts and think about how you don't know for sure if you put the confidential materials away. By doing this exercise repeatedly, you will see that you are able to manage your distress better than you thought, even if you don't go back and check or try to mentally review your activities to reassure yourself. The goal is for you to learn that you can live your life even if these obsessional doubts are there.

For this imaginal exposure, I will ask you to write a script in which you describe what you're afraid would happen if your worst fears come true. We will then make a recording of this script so that you can listen to it over and over. Every 5 minutes you can say your SUDS rating to track your anxiety level. Your job will be to "bring on" the anxiety and uncertainty so you can learn that these thoughts and feelings are manageable for you.

The patient then wrote a description of his feared consequences of leaving confidential materials on his desk and failing to check. The description was edited with the therapist to ensure that it contained elements that the patient experienced as most distressing, such as his irresponsibility for the breach of confidentiality, and the idea that he *should* have checked more carefully. The script was then recorded so that the patient could focus on it and visualize the scene until he had tolerated the distress and uncertainty for longer than he predicted he could. By doing this, he learned that he could manage this obsessional distress.

Unacceptable Obsessional Thoughts

Using imaginal exposure for repugnant obsessional thoughts

ERP for unacceptable thoughts involves exposure to external cues that trigger these obsessions, as well as imaginal exposure to obsessional thoughts and images themselves. Such exposures are repeated in multiple contexts to generalize learning. The example in Vignette 12 illustrates how to conduct an exposure session for a patient with repugnant stabbing obsessions.

Clinical Vignette 12
Introducing an Exposure Exercise for Unacceptable Obsessional Thoughts

Therapist: The exercise you will do for today's exposure will help you become better at managing your thoughts about stabbing people and the anxiety that comes with these thoughts. We will start by having you write a description of the obsessional thoughts, which we will record and you will practice listening to the recording. You will also practice holding sharp objects, like a knife. Remember that we are working on not trying to fight or control these thoughts, so it will be important that you don't make any attempt to suppress, remove, or neutralize them. If you do feel yourself trying to remove the thought, let me know so I can help you remain exposed. The goal of this exercise is not to make the thoughts go away, but to give you the opportunity to learn to relate to them in a healthier way. I will keep track of your SUDS during the exercise.

The patient was first asked to write a script of her obsessional thoughts. After editing with the therapist (to highlight the most distressing aspects), the final version, which the patient audio recorded, was as follows:

Sharp objects can be dangerous. I could use them to stab people, which would badly hurt or kill them. When I use knives, I often think of stabbing innocent people and people that I especially care about, like my husband, Greg. If people are not expecting to be stabbed, I could do terrible damage with just a few thrusts of a knife in the right place, such as their neck, eyes, chest, stomach, or genitals. If a person is not ready, they would not be able to fight back until it was too late and they would die of their stab wounds that I inflicted.

I could stab Greg while he was sleeping. He would be unaware that I was doing it until the knife pierced his skin and entered his body. He might wake up in terror and try to fight off my stabbing, but he would lose so much blood that he wouldn't be able to fight me off. I could easily kill him by stabbing him in his sleep. There would be blood everywhere and he would be screaming from all of the pain. If I stabbed him in the right place, I'd damage his vital organs and he would die.

The patient predicted that she could only tolerate having this thought for 10 min without neutralizing because her distress would be "too high." So, exposure involved testing this out. After she was able to confront the thought for over 20 min with her SUDS at 90, the therapist helped her consolidate what she learned so far – that she could tolerate the obsession and feelings of anxiety better than she thought. After that point, with her SUDS decreasing only to 75, the therapist gave the patient a large butcher knife and asked her to hold it while listening to the recording. After an initial increase in SUDS back to 90, she was able to remain exposed without neutralizing for another 20 min. The therapist then introduced the patient to a coworker (another therapist who had volunteered to help with treatment). The recording was turned off and the patient was asked to hold the knife while talking with this confederate. Then, the confederate sat at a computer terminal while the patient held the knife to the confederate's back and elicited stabbing thoughts. Finally, this exercise was continued with the therapist out of the room, but checking in every 5 min to obtain a SUDS rating. The exposure was ended after 60 min and the patient and therapist discussed what had been learned in terms of tolerance of obsessions and anxiety. The patient's SUDS was 70 when the exposure was ended, but she was confident that she could tolerate the anxiety.

Incompleteness Symptoms

Patients with incompleteness symptoms may or may not articulate fears of harm. When the sense of inexactness, imperfection, or asymmetry evoke obsessional fears of responsibility for disasters (e.g., "Dad will die if I do not put on my clothes the 'correct' way"), exposure to external cues should be conducted, accompanied by imaginal exposure to the feared consequences (as with harming obsessions). Remind patients to refrain from rituals such as ordering and arranging, checking and repeating, and reassurance-seeking. One patient who worried that stepping on sidewalk cracks would cause harm to his parents purposely stepped on cracks and confronted thoughts of his parents being injured because of this. Another feared bad luck from odd numbers and therefore practiced facing them wherever possible by purchasing items that cost $7.99, and choosing to be ninth in line. He also practiced wishing for bad luck to occur as a result of his confrontation with odd numbers.

When the patient is mostly concerned that feelings of anxiety and the sense that something is "not-just-right" will persist indefinitely unless rituals are performed, exposure aims to change beliefs about one's ability to tolerate these uncomfortable feelings while they are present. With prolonged and repeated exposure to the "imperfection," the patient learns that the distress associated with these feelings is manageable, thereby rendering ordering rituals unnecessary.

Integrating cognitive techniques into exposure therapy

Clinical Pearl
Integrating Cognitive Therapy With Exposure

Exposure exercises help the patient develop more realistic estimates of the probability and severity of feared consequences. The patient's ability to exceed his or her expectations of what he or she can handle also helps to modify maladaptive beliefs that anxiety, uncertainty, and other negative feelings that accompany obsessions are intolerable or will persist indefinitely. Cognitive therapy techniques can be used at various points during exposure sessions to facilitate these cognitive changes.

- **When initiating an exposure task**, cognitive techniques can be used to identify mistaken cognitions (e.g., "thinking about harm is the same as causing harm") and feared consequences (e.g., "I will be responsible for a terrible accident") that can be tested during exposure.

- **During exposures**, cognitive techniques can be used to promote adaptive beliefs and responses to obsessional fear (e.g., "Even if something happens, it's not my fault").

- **After an exposure exercise**, Socratic discussion is used to help the patient review the outcome of the exercise, examine evidence for and against the original catastrophic beliefs, and develop more realistic beliefs about obsessional stimuli.

Prescribing Homework Practice

At the completion of each in-session exposure, assign practices for each day between sessions. Homework includes (1) exposure practice, (2) refraining from rituals and neutralizing, and (3) continual self-monitoring of rituals that cannot be resisted. Consider the following points when designing homework assignments:

- Assign repetitions and variations of the in-session situational and imaginal exposure exercises.
- The more exposure is practiced under different conditions and in different situations, the better.
- Provide copies of the Exposure Practice Form to be completed during each homework assignment. Specify the details of each assignment and be sure the patient knows how to complete the form properly.
- Suggest that the patient review The Guidelines for Conducting Exposure handout.
- Reinforce the importance of homework by beginning each session with a check of the previously assigned work.

Planning for the Next Session

At the end of each session, the therapist should review the patient's progress and discuss the task scheduled for the next session, including whether it is going to be randomly selected. If items need to be brought from the patient's home, or if the session must take place out of the office, this should be arranged.

Conclude each treatment session by reviewing progress and discussing plans for the next session's exposure exercise

Conducting Exposure to Very Distressing Stimuli

Although patients will likely be hesitant to confront exposure items that provoke a great deal of anxiety and fear, learning that even high levels of anxiety are manageable is important for long-term improvement. Accordingly, try to strike a balance between encouraging patients to push themselves (i.e., a "bring it on" attitude) and letting them decide when they are ready. Consider that procrastination on the patient's part might be a form of avoidance. It can be helpful to review educational materials about the nature of anxiety (e.g., the fight-flight response is a normal and adaptive process that is not dangerous). It is important to use such exposures to target the patient's beliefs about his or her ability to tolerate anxiety along with beliefs about obsessionally feared consequences. Be sure to allow time to repeat these exposures in varied contexts since fear extinction is most complete and long-lasting when feared stimuli are confronted in a variety of circumstances, as opposed to only in the therapist's office.

Clinical Pearl
Helping Patients Confront Their Greatest Fears

You can use the following tactics to help patients who are having difficulty attempting the most difficult exposures:

- Model the task prior to instructing the patient to engage.
- Use intermediate exposures that are of greater difficulty than those already conducted, but not as difficult as the planned task (the patient should agree that the intermediate step serves to facilitate eventual exposure with the more difficult item).
- Use Socratic dialogue to help the patient challenge maladaptive beliefs about the dangerousness and tolerability of anxiety.
- Review evidence collected during previous exposures.
- Discuss the importance of learning to take acceptable risks.
- Revisit the importance of learning to tolerate uncertainty

Programmed and Lifestyle Exposure: Encouraging Independence

The illustrations of ERP in this chapter primarily illustrate *programmed* expo-sure in which the patient implements planned exercises under your direction (e.g., at specific times and in particular locations). Yet it is also important for patients to engage in *lifestyle* exposure, which means making choices to take advantage of any opportunities to practice confronting (rather than avoiding) obsessional stimuli and choosing to tolerate anxiety, especially if these arise dur-ing valued activities. Encourage the patent to be opportunistic and view spon-taneously arising obsessional triggers as occasions to practice persisting with important activities while developing a healthier relationship with obsessions.

You should routinely remind patients that every choice they make regard-ing whether to confront or avoid an obsessional cue carries weight. Each time they choose to confront such a situation without using rituals, they are strengthening new learning that will lead to long-term OCD symptom reduc-tion. Yet, whenever a decision is made to avoid a potential lifestyle exposure, they are reinforcing their OCD-related fears.

As it becomes clear that the patient has learned to correctly implement exposure independently, step back and encourage "becoming your own thera-pist." This means allowing the patient to design his or her own exposure tasks to help prepare the patient for life after therapy. Of course, the therapist has the last word regarding the nature of each exercise, and you must therefore monitor the planning and implementation of these tasks.

Stylistic Considerations

Remarks During Exposure Tasks

Offering appropriate observations, praise, encouragement, and support dur-ing exposure maintains the sort of rapport that is necessary for a successful outcome. Encourage the patient to describe out loud what he or she is thinking and feeling. Also, foster abundant conversation about what is being learned by doing exposures. When exercises are proceeding as planned, the following sorts of comments and open-ended questions can be helpful:

- "You're doing great. Remember, when you remain exposed to a situa-tion, you learn that you can manage it."
- "It looks like you're much less anxious now compared to when we started the session, and you haven't done any rituals. How do you explain that your anxiety is lower?"
- "This seems like it's getting easier for you. You're learning that obses-sional thoughts and anxiety aren't as awful as you thought. Good for you."
- "You see, as we talked about before, you don't need to engage in rituals to get through this situation."

If the patient is having difficulty with anxiety during the exercise, convey understanding of how difficult exposure can be, and that with time and persis-tence the exercises will become more manageable. Offer the following remarks:

- "It's important to stick with the exposure even though it is difficult. You can do this! I know you can manage feeling the anxiety. You'll be glad you stuck with it."

- "Yes, the anxiety (fear, uncertainty, distress) is unpleasant and uncomfortable, but you can tolerate it. You can get through it. I have confidence in you!"
- "This time your anxiety did not decrease by much, but you still learned that anxiety does not have to go down for you to live your life. This is a very important lesson."

Avoid providing reassurance that exposure tasks are "not dangerous," that safety is assured, or that anxiety will definitely go down. These are things that cannot be guaranteed and that exposure allows the patient to test (and learn) for him- or herself. The example below illustrates a helpful and unhelpful way to address patient requests for reassurance during exposure.

What to say (and what *not* to say) during exposure sessions

Patient: Are you sure this is safe to do? Normal people wouldn't do a thing like this!

Unhelpful therapist response: Yes, it's OK. I promise. I wouldn't let anything bad happen to you. Just trust me.

Helpful therapist response: If you are asking me to guarantee you that the situation is absolutely safe, I can't do that. I can't even say for certain what the outcome will be. But I do know that all the evidence suggests that the risk is low enough that it's worth testing out; especially if doing this exercise will help with your OCD …

Dealing With Strong Urges to Ritualize

As patients begin response prevention, they may have difficulty with strong urges to ritualize. Reviewing how such urges are learned responses to obsessional cues, and how they are tolerable if resisted, is useful in helping the patient refrain from rituals. The use of imagery can also be helpful, as in the example in Clinical Vignette 13 about a patient who struggled with resisting compulsive urges to check door locks in her home.

Clinical Vignette 13

Using Imagery to Manage Compulsive Urges

Therapist: Is there something you could imagine — it doesn't matter what the image is — that will grab you and help you resist? Perhaps you could imagine spraying the urge with a fire extinguisher, or surfing on the urge until it crests and breaks.

Patient: [Smiling] I know what I can imagine — I could picture you standing in front of the door, waving your finger and shaking your head at me.

Therapist: That's great. Should I look mean?

Patient: No, just having you there will help me stop checking.

Therapist: That sounds like a good plan.

Humor

The use of humor or laughter to lighten the mood during exposures may be appropriate and can be beneficial, although being playful is not always best in times of extreme distress. Follow the patient's lead, and ensure that remarks are relevant to the exposure situation and do not distract the patient from the task.

Refining the Exposure List

Sometimes important details of the patient's obsessional fears do not become apparent until after the exposure list has been developed. Therefore, as treatment progresses, the therapist should remain alert for previously unidentified situations and stimuli that trigger obsessions, avoidance, or that evoke compulsive rituals. Such situations should be incorporated into the exposure list.

Exposure "Field Trips"

The highly specific obsessions and avoidance behaviors of individuals with OCD often require that exposure exercises be conducted outside of the therapist's office. Such "field trips" might include visiting funeral homes, cemeteries, restaurants, places of worship, hospitals, stores, the patient's own home, driving, etc. Ideally, the therapist has the flexibility to leave the office or meet the patient at the site where such exposures can take place. If not, a well-coached support person could accompany the patient on such trips. A final option is for the patient to check in with the therapist by phone while conducting the exposure tasks on his or her own.

Usually, exposures in public places can be conducted anonymously. The therapist and patient should plan in advance how the exercise will proceed so that directives can be kept to a minimum in public. Necessary behaviors such as touching or rearranging items should be performed discreetly so as not to draw undue attention. Unforeseen difficulties, such as high levels of anxiety or a persistent sales clerk, can be managed by leaving the scene, regrouping, and returning another time. In some situations it may be ideal to call ahead before visiting exposure situations. For example, one of the authors asked a patient to call ahead to let a funeral home manager that we would be dropping by. The patient explained that the purpose of this visit was to help her overcome her fears of funerals. When a cover story and plans for various contingencies (e.g., running into a friend) are discussed ahead of time, we find that most patients are willing to go out in public to conduct exposures with their therapist.

4.1.8   Ending Treatment

This section discusses a number of issues that should be addressed toward the end of therapy.

Deciding on When to End Treatment

The following are often signs that it is appropriate to consider ending treatment in the near future:

- The patient is able to completely (or almost completely) refrain from rituals.
- The patient is able to design and implement exposures with no (or minimal) therapist input or guidance.
- The patient's daily routine is not (or only minimally) adversely impacted by OCD symptoms.

Concluding Response Prevention

As the last session nears, begin to discuss appropriate checking, cleaning, arranging, or praying behavior. As a rule, if such behaviors are performed in response to fears of negative consequences, they are probably rituals. Some examples of guidelines for resuming "normal" behavior after treatment appear below.

Helping the patient end response prevention and return to "normal" behavior

- Limit showering to one 10-min shower per day. A second shower is permitted if there is extreme perspiration and body odor, or before getting dressed to go out (e.g., to a formal event). During any shower, wash each body part only once.
- Once the door is closed, you are allowed to turn the handle once to make sure it is firmly locked. Otherwise, no returning to check is allowed.

Assessing Treatment Outcome

In addition to informally assessing progress, evaluation of treatment outcome should include readministration of symptom measures (e.g., DOCS) and measures of general functioning (e.g., the Sheehan Disability Scale; Sheehan, 1983). Most patients will report some residual symptoms and impairment. Emphasize that "normal" obsessions and rituals are a part of everyday life for most people, so such experiences will likely never completely be absent. However, treatment has aimed to help the patient learn to respond to obsessional stimuli in new healthy ways while continuing to engage in life's activities. Distress and functional impairment can be minimized with continued practice of the skills learned in treatment.

Obtain posttreatment ratings of symptom severity to accurately document progress in treatment

Continuing Care

Some patients desire additional treatment. As a general rule, those who have made little progress after 16–20 sessions of well-conducted CBT are unlikely to benefit further by adding additional sessions at that time, and might consider taking a break from therapy and returning at a later date. Attending a support group run by a local affiliate of the International Obsessive-Compulsive Disorder Foundation (http://www.iocdf.org), if available, is another good option. If residual OCD symptoms are minimal, yet there is concern about possible relapse, follow-up sessions can be considered. Alternatively, a less formal strategy involving telephone calls and less frequent (perhaps monthly) appointments could be undertaken.

Preparing for Stressors

Patients should *expect* to experience residual OCD symptoms from time to time. Often, these are triggered by increased life stress, such as in the midst of occupational or family conflict, following a death or serious illness in the family, travelling, or around the time of childbirth. Help the patient identify potential "high risk" periods during which they should be ready to apply the techniques learned in therapy.

4.2   Mechanisms of Action

From a learning theory perspective, ERP provides an opportunity for the extinction of conditioned fear responses. This theory views obsessional thoughts (and their triggers) as conditioned stimuli that provoke fear as a conditioned response; and avoidance, compulsive rituals, and other safety cues, as strategies for managing obsessional fear that are negatively reinforced by the reduction in distress they engender. Traditionally the efficacy of ERP was understood in terms of emotional processing theory (EPT; Foa, Huppert, & Cahill, 2006; Foa & Kozak, 1986), which credits initial fear activation followed by habituation (both within and between sessions) as the mechanisms of improvement. The basic assumptions of EPT, however, are not well supported by the research evidence (Craske et al., 2014): Successful habituation during exposure often fails to predict long-term outcomes, and successful outcomes can occur in the absence of habituation.

Inhibitory learning is a proposed mechanism of fear extinction

Numerous developments in research on learning and memory relevant to exposure and extinction point to *inhibitory learning* as the mechanism of extinction (e.g., Craske et al., 2014). From the inhibitory learning perspective, the original danger-based association between the conditioned and unconditioned stimulus (e.g., "floors cause sickness," and "uncertainty about the future is intolerable") remain intact during exposure, while competing nondanger-based associations (e.g., "floors are generally safe," "Uncertainty is manageable") are formed. The goal of ERP for OCD, then, is to optimize the likelihood that the new nondanger associations will inhibit access to and retrieval of the old threat associations. In other words, the goal is to maximize the strength, durability, and generalization of the learning that takes place during exposure. The degree to which threat-based versus nonthreat-based associations are expressed after finishing treatment depends on the strength of inhibitory learning across time and in different contexts. The descriptions and illustrations of ERP in this chapter incorporate numerous techniques and suggestions for maximizing inhibitory learning (e.g., Craske et al., 2014).

Increasing tolerance of fear, uncertainty, and disgust also has clinical value in treating OCD, and complements the goal of inhibitory learning. To the degree that distress is tolerated (e.g., "Anxiety and uncertainty are a part of life, so I'm better off learning to accept that I can't know for sure if every building I enter is 100% asbestos free"), inhibitory associations can be more robustly acquired ("If fear is tolerable, then I can push myself to go into older buildings and learn that I can manage this acceptable risk"). Increasing tolerance for experiences such as fear, disgust, and uncertainty also reduces the likelihood that an inevitable unexpected encounter with one of these experiences in a new context (e.g., once treatment has ended) will lead to the return of fear and relapse.

From a cognitive perspective, ERP corrects maladaptive beliefs that underlie OCD symptoms (e.g., overestimates of threat) by presenting the patient with information that disconfirms these beliefs. Cognitive and educational interventions aim to modify such cognitions via a verbal-linguistic route, whereas ERP accomplishes the same goal experientially. CBT also facilitates self-efficacy by helping patients master their fears and continue to engage in everyday life without having to rely on avoidance or safety behaviors.

4.3   Efficacy and Prognosis

Numerous research trials evaluating the efficacy of exposure-based CBT for OCD consistently show that patients who complete this treatment achieve clinically significant and durable improvement. Average improvement rates are typically from 50 to 70% in these studies (Olatunji, Davis, Powers, & Smits, 2013). A review of 16 trials (involving 756 patients) indicated that CBT was substantially more effective than comparison treatments (e.g., relaxation, anxiety management training, waiting list, medication) immediately following therapy (effect size = 1.39) and moderately more effective at long-term follow-up (effect size = 0.43; Olatunji et al., 2013). These trials indicate that the effects of CBT are due to the specific cognitive and behavioral techniques (i.e., exposure and response prevention) over and above any effects of nonspecific factors common to all interventions, such as the therapeutic relationship and spontaneous improvement. Moreover, the effects of CBT are not limited to highly selected research samples or to treatment as delivered in specialty clinics. *Effectiveness studies* conducted with nonresearch patients (e.g., Franklin, Abramowitz, Foa, Kozak, & Levitt, 2000) show that over 80% of patients who complete CBT achieve clinically significant improvement. While CBT is effective for most people with OCD, about 20% do not respond and about 25–30% drop out of therapy. Factors associated with poor outcome (e.g., severe depression) are discussed in Section 3.4.

There is excellent scientific evidence of the effectiveness of CBT for OCD

4.4   Variations and Combinations of Methods

4.4.1   Variants of CBT Treatment Procedures

There is a relationship between treatment outcome and how CBT is delivered along four parameters. First, better short- and long-term outcome is achieved when treatment involves in-session exposure practice that is supervised by a therapist, as compared to when all exposure is performed by the patient as homework assignments. In fact, the number of hours of therapist-directed exposure is positively correlated with outcome. Second, combining situational and imaginal exposure is superior to situational exposure alone. Third, programs in which patients completely refrain from rituals during the treatment period produce superior immediate and long-term effects compared to those that involve only partial response prevention. Finally, compliance with instructions to practice exposure assignments between sessions is a predictor of positive outcome, which highlights the importance of exposure practice outside the session.

   In addition, it is essential that patients understand the rationale for using the various CBT techniques discussed in this book. Patients will be able to better apply and maximize benefit from ERP when they comprehend the conceptual basis for these strategies.

4.4.2   Combining Medication and CBT

The concurrent use of CBT and SRI medication for OCD is common in clinical settings. The available research indicates that whereas adding CBT to SRIs yields superior outcome compared to SRIs alone, adding SRIs neither improves nor attenuates the efficacy of CBT (e.g., Foa et al., 2005). Thus, CBT is an excellent augmentation strategy for individuals with OCD who remain symptomatic despite adequate trials of SRI medications (but not necessarily the other way around).

4.4.3   Involving Significant Others in Treatment

For patients involved in close relationships (e.g., who are married), involving a significant other in ERP can have benefits; especially if the patient is having difficulty completing exposure on his or her own. The partner should attend treatment sessions, be socialized to the treatment approach, and be taught how to assist with exposure exercises by serving as a coach. This role includes offering emotional support to the patient and providing gentle, but firm reminders not to ritualize. Train the partner to ensure that fears are adequately tested, and rituals resisted, during exposures. Emphasize helping the patient "get through" the obsessional anxiety, as opposed to the partner trying to immediately alleviate this distress.

In their couple-based CBT program for OCD, Abramowitz et al. (2013) divide the process of partner-assisted exposure into four phases and incorporate communication skills at each phase to help couples complete the exercises as a team. In session with the couple, you can introduce the four phases and then work through an exposure as follows:

Phase 1: Discussing the exposure task. Begin by helping the patient and partner clarify the specifics of the exposure task. Both parties are encouraged to discuss how each is feeling about the upcoming practice and to identify potential obstacles. The patient is helped to specify how he or she would like the partner to help with the exercise.

Phase 2: Confronting the feared situation. Encourage the patient to express his or her feelings to the partner, who listens carefully and reflects these feelings (as opposed to offering advice or solutions; e.g., "I can tell that you're feeling anxious about this exposure). If the patient becomes anxious, the partner acknowledges this and uses praise to reinforce the patient's hard work (e.g., "You're doing great. I'm really proud of you!"). The partner continues to compliment the patient on handling the situation throughout the exercise, and avoids making negative statements. The partner also resists the temptation to distract the patient or provide reassurance or any other anxiety reduction strategies.

Phase 3: Dealing with overwhelming anxiety. If the patient experiences extreme distress, teach him or her to let the partner know. In turn, teach the partner to acknowledge that exposure is difficult but that the patient can get through it. If the patient absolutely cannot continue with the exposure, a brief timeout can be taken during which the partner provides support in ways the patient would like (but *not* using reassurance, rituals, or accommodation behaviors). The two parties also discuss what went wrong and how they can approach resuming the exposure.

Phase 4: Evaluation. Help the parties to evaluate how the exposure went. How did the patient feel about the experience and the partner's coaching? The partner should also let the patient know how he or she felt and, when appropriate, provide praise for a job well done.

For many partners, assisting with ERP and seeing a loved one experience significant anxiety is upsetting. In a manner of speaking, the partner is undergoing a form of ERP as well – allowing the patient's distress to continue rather than reducing it by accommodation. Consequently, it is important to support the partner as well, both for being an effective coach and for tolerating the patient's distress. Additional details regarding couple-based CBT for OCD can be found in Abramowitz et al. (2013).

4.5   Problems in Carrying Out the Treatment

Table 12 lists common problems that arise during CBT for OCD. Suggestions for managing such obstacles are provided below.

Table 12
Common Obstacles in Cognitive-Behavior Therapy for OCD

- Negative reactions to the CBT model
- Nonadherence
  - Noncompliance with exposure instructions
  - Noncompliance with response prevention instructions
  - Continued use of avoidance and subtle rituals
- Arguments
- Family accommodation
- Therapist's inclination to challenge the obsession
- Hijacking psychoeducational and cognitive therapy techniques
- Using exposure to control anxiety

4.5.1   Negative Reactions to the CBT Model

Some patients hold the belief that OCD symptoms are caused by a genetic, neurobiological disturbance, or "chemical imbalance," and therefore "talk therapy" won't be helpful. Because negative reactions to the CBT model can lead to premature discontinuation, any doubts about the CBT model should be discussed. Highlight that the CBT model was developed to explain the *symptoms* of OCD, not necessarily its causes (therefore, the CBT approach is not incompatible with a biological approach). You might also point out that studies show CBT has effects on brain functioning.

4.5.2 Nonadherence

The degree of improvement obtained in cbt is often directly related to how well the patient adheres to the treatment instructions

The most common obstacle encountered in CBT for OCD is the patient's failure to follow through with treatment instructions. Many adherence problems can be circumvented by ensuring that the patient clearly understands the rationale for using these techniques. On occasion, this information needs to be reviewed with patients. You should also actively involve the patient in the treatment planning process.

Noncompliance With Exposure

If a patient refuses to complete exposure tasks (e.g., homework assignments), inquire as to why this is. Sometimes the problem can be addressed with simple problem solving (e.g., time management). Also, make sure the exposure task itself is a good match to the patient's obsessional fears. If not, the patient might perceive the exercise as irrelevant. If high levels of anxiety prompt refusal or "shortcuts" (e.g., subtle avoidance, rituals) during exposure, review the treatment rationale and emphasize that an important goal of treatment is anxiety tolerance. Cognitive strategies can also be used to identify and address maladaptive beliefs about anxiety that might underlie reluctance to confront the feared stimulus (e.g., anxiety will persist forever and spiral out of control).

Modifying the exposure list and adding items the patient would be willing to try might be appropriate if the patient threatens to discontinue treatment. Postpone exposures only as a last resort because doing so can reinforce avoidance. Instead, start a discussion about the patient's goals for treatment and how postponing exposures may conflict with values the patient wishes to pursue (such as self-image, happiness, success, being able to spend more time with friends and family). When a lack of progress in treatment is perceived as conflicting with important personal goals, it can increase motivation for change.

Noncompliance With Response Prevention

If the patient is deliberately concealing ritualistic behavior that was specifically targeted in the treatment plan, explain the implications of this problem for treatment outcome in the following way:

> Therapist: *Your wife emailed to tell me that you changed your clothes several times last weekend after going in the basement. She felt I needed to be aware of this because she was concerned that you weren't following the instructions we all agreed to at the beginning of therapy. We discussed that if problems come up, you were going to get help from your wife instead of doing rituals. Let's talk about this.*

If the patient makes a renewed agreement to adhere to the treatment instructions, the issue can be dropped. However, if repeated infractions occur, remind the patient of the rationale for response prevention and raise the possibility that now is not the best time to undergo treatment. For example:

> Therapist: It seems that right now you aren't able to stop your rituals as we had agreed at the beginning of treatment. Remember that each time you do a ritual you are preventing yourself from learning that you can tolerate the

obsessional distress. If this is too difficult for you right now, perhaps this is not the right time for you to be doing this kind of treatment.

Continued Use of Avoidance and Subtle Rituals

Patients sometimes adopt covert tactics for avoiding or neutralizing obsessional distress even after stopping their overt rituals. Examples include the use of brief actions (e.g., quickly wiping hands instead of washing) or mental rituals (e.g., instead of asking for reassurance). Although the patient might not realize that these behaviors are interfering with treatment, they are functionally equivalent to overt compulsive rituals: they interfere with learning to manage obsessional situations and internal experiences (e.g., anxiety). Periodically inquire about such "mini rituals," especially if highly anticipated exposures seem to be "easy" for patients. For example, "Now that you've stopped your compulsive rituals, are you doing any other little things to relieve anxiety?"

4.5.3   Arguments

Some patients become argumentative about the "strictness" of response prevention rules or the "dangerousness" or "normality" of exposure tasks. You should resist the urge to lecture the patient using logic (e.g., by appealing to probabilities), and instead use Socratic methods so that the belief-altering information is generated by the patient him or herself.

> It is important to avoid arguing with patients about the treatment instructions

In the example in Clinical Vignette 14, the patient argues that speaking *one more time* with an infectious disease expert (Dr. B) would terminate his need for reassurance about the risk of catching AIDS from public restrooms:

Clinical Vignette 14
The Use of Socratic Dialogue to Address Patient Arguments

Patient: I just have to ask Dr. B one more question about catching AIDS from public toilets. I can't go on without asking.

Therapist: I understand that you are anxious about this. Let's talk about that decision, though. You know that would be a compulsive ritual that we are trying to stop.

Patient: But I need to know. I might have put myself at risk of catching AIDS. You don't understand. I'm so worried.

Therapist: What has Dr. B told you in the past when you've asked her about these kinds of situations?

Patient: That I'm not likely to catch AIDS that way. But this time it's different. I really feel like I could have AIDS. Please, just one more time. I have to ask her.

Therapist: Oh, so each time you've asked Dr. B about AIDS she tells you that you probably have nothing to worry about. That's interesting. What do you think she'll say to you this time?

Patient: I hadn't thought about it that way before. You're right. She'll probably tell me the same thing.

Therapist: OK, so if you already think you know what she'll say, would you agree that the only reason for asking her again is just to hear her say it so that your anxiety and uncertainty is relieved?

Patient: I guess so.

> **Therapist:** Then wouldn't it be more helpful for you to use this opportunity to learn that you can tolerate this uncertainty and anxiety rather than always having to ask Dr. B. for reassurances whenever you think about AIDS? After all, we've discussed how the reassurance-seeking only makes OCD stronger because it only works temporarily.
>
> **Patient:** Yes. You're right. I see what you mean.

If discussions about the risks associated with exposure tasks become combative, summarize the discussion and agree with the patient that his or her assertion *could* be correct (i.e., agree that some risk does exist); but that rather than analyzing the level of risk, it is better to practice managing uncertainty (e.g., using exposure). Do your best to refrain from debates over probability or the degree of risk. Such arguments reinforce the patient's OCD patterns of spending too much time thinking about these issues, and they amount to little more than a playing out of the patient's fruitless (ritualistic) attempts to gain reassurance. Moreover, when patients perceive that the therapist is frustrated, angry, or coercive, they often lose motivation (e.g., "you can't make me do this"). Instead, step back and recognize that the decision to engage in treatment is a difficult one.

Clinical Pearl
When the Patient Argues

When a patient becomes argumentative (e.g., during exposure), it might indicate a rising level of distress. Instead of engaging in arguments about risk or "what is normal," the best strategy is identify the problem and ask the patient what he or she might suggest for resolving it. Have in mind how much it is useful to modify the therapy instructions without compromising treatment. Statements such as the following might also be helpful:

- You are here in treatment for yourself – not for me. So, I won't argue or debate with you. Doing the treatment is entirely your choice. You stand to get better by trying these exercises and learning how to handle the anxiety. But you are also the one who has to live with the OCD symptoms if you choose not to do the therapy.
- Remember that we both agreed on the treatment plan. I hope you will hold up your end of the bargain.
- I agree with you that there is *some* risk involved; but it is acceptable risk. The goal of treatment is to help you learn that you can be OK even in situations where it is impossible to have a complete guarantee of safety.
- I realize *most* people wouldn't go out of their way to do what I am asking you to do. But the therapy isn't about what people *usually* do. These tasks are designed to help you learn to manage acceptable levels of risk and uncertainty.
- I know this is a difficult decision for you. Yet, if you are going to get over OCD, you have to confront your uncertainty and find out that you can manage the risk.

4.5.4   Persistent Family Accommodation of OCD Symptoms

Accommodation can hinder treatment outcome

Accommodation of OCD symptoms by an intimate partner, other relative, or friend can hinder treatment outcome. If this is occurring, work with the patient and accommodating individual together to help them change these interaction patterns. Describe accommodation and its deleterious effects, noting that such behavior is often is well intended (as we discuss earlier in this book). Then, help the parties to choose an activity which has become hampered by OCD symptoms, and facilitate a discussion about ways to handle this situation by promoting the idea of exposure and fear tolerance, rather than relying on avoidance and compulsive rituals. In other words, help the parties build ERP techniques into their relationship. For example, a husband might resume using various rooms in the house that had been off limits. A wife might stop checking doors and windows for her husband with OCD prior to coming to bed. The goal of these interventions is to work toward a life in which the individuals confront the situations and stimuli that the person with OCD has been avoiding to practice experiencing the anxiety.

When encouraging a loved one not to accommodate a patient's OCD symptoms, it is important to understand what function the accommodation plays in the relationship and address these issues. For example, accommodation might have become a major way that a husband shows care, concern, and love for his wife. Keep an eye out for situations in which removing accommodation changes the relationship such that the parties feel less close to each other, or the patient does not feel as loved by the partner. Discuss with the couple what new ways they want to show their love, care, and concern for each other, instead of through accommodation of OCD symptoms.

4.5.5 Therapist's Inclination to Challenge the Obsession

Therapists occasionally fall into the trap of challenging the logic of patients' obsessional thoughts (e.g., "the impulse to attack an elderly person") rather than challenging the patient's faulty beliefs *about* the obsessions. Clinical Vignette 15 highlights the distinction between these two approaches (Examples 1 and 2).

Intuitively, the obsession itself seems like a good target for cognitive techniques because it is a cognitive event and it is irrational. Yet, most patients already recognize the irrationality of their obsessions. So, direct challenges will have only a transient therapeutic effect. Moreover, such challenges could turn into reassurance-seeking strategies used to neutralize the obsession. In contrast, challenging the *appraisal* of the obsession gives the patient new information that is different from reassurance.

Another option is to use ACT metaphors (e.g., Passengers on the Bus) to help the patient gain some distance from his or her thoughts and see them as *thoughts*, not *facts*. Example 3 in Vignette 15 illustrates this option.

Clinical Vignette 15
Challenging Obsessions

Example 1: Challenging the obsession
Therapist: Which intrusive thoughts have been particular problems for you this week?
Patient: Every time I am around my grandfather, I get these terrible images of attacking him. He's a frail old man, and I love him very much. But I can't stop thinking about beating him.

Therapist: Let's look at the evidence. What do you think the likelihood is that you will beat your grandfather?

Patient: Pretty low. I've never done it before even though I've thought about it a lot.

Example 2: Challenging faulty appraisals and beliefs

Therapist: Which intrusive thoughts have been particular problems for you this week?

Patient: Every time I am around my grandfather, I get these terrible images of attacking him. He's a frail old man, and I love him very much. But I can't stop thinking about beating him.

Therapist: When these kinds of thoughts come up, how do you interpret them? What do they mean to you?

Patient: They mean that I am a terrible person deep down. I mean who the hell thinks of killing their own grandfather!? I need to be careful that I don't do anything awful, so I avoid him.

Therapist: Let's look more closely at your beliefs about these unwanted thoughts. Where is the evidence that because you have violent thoughts, you're really a violent person? What do we know about who has violent thoughts?

Patient: Well, you taught me that once in a while everyone has thoughts like I do. So, maybe these thoughts aren't as dangerous as I'm thinking they are.

Example 3: Using an ACT metaphor

Therapist: Which intrusive thoughts have been particular problems for you this week?

Patient: Every time I am around my grandfather, I get these terrible images of attacking him. He's a frail old man, and I love him very much. But I can't stop thinking about beating him.

Therapist: Sounds like you've got some really nasty passengers on the bus this week. What are they yelling at you now?

Patient: They're saying that I am a terrible person deep down because I'm thinking about killing my own grandfather. And they're saying I need to be careful that I don't do anything awful, and that I need to I avoid him.

Therapist: It sounds like you've got some options. You can pull the bus over and argue with the passengers; you could just drive the bus where they want to go so that they'll quiet down for you; or you could keep driving the bus in the direction you want to go – toward spending quality time with family – and just let the passengers yell at you. What do you want to do?

Patient: I guess I need to keep driving if I'm going to beat this problem. Spending time with my family is really important to me.

4.5.6 Hijacking Psychoeducational and Cognitive Interventions

Watch out for patients "hijacking" psychoeducational and cognitive interventions

Some patients convert discussions about mistaken beliefs into reassurance seeking rituals. For example, one patient ritualistically repeated (three times perfectly) the phrase "obsessional thoughts are normal" to reduce anxiety associated with his unwanted sexual images before feeling "ready" to begin an exposure. Others become preoccupied with identifying the *perfect* rational belief that *best* reassures them that feared consequences are impossible. The best way to sidestep these problems is to amplify uncertainty and maintain the focus on tolerance of this feeling. For example, stress that even the most perfect rational belief is still a guess and not a guarantee.

As a general rule, if the patient uses psychoeducational information in a stereotypic way, or requires increasing clarification, the material is probably being used as a ritual. In contrast, healthy use of cognitive techniques and education results in long-term changes in behavior and allows the patient to developing a healthier relationship with obsessional stimuli that leads to acting appropriately during exposure.

4.5.7   Using Exposure to Control Anxiety

If patients see the point of exposure too narrowly as a means of reducing anxiety via habituation, it can lead to using exposure techniques as another anxiety control strategy (i.e., functionally equivalent to rituals) that, ironically, will interfere with treatment response. Signs of this include patients seeming relieved when exposure practices are finished, saying that they "know anxiety will go down by the time the exposure is over," and describing their use of exposure (or its goal) as a way of lessening anxiety. Emphasizing habituation as a goal of exposure can increase the chances of patients exploiting exposure in this way. To minimize the likelihood of this occurrence, emphasize that the aim of exposure is to practice confronting anxiety, intrusive thoughts, and uncertainty to learn that such emotions are tolerable – not to reduce them. In other words, the aim is to help the patient "become *better* at anxiety, not *reduce* it." Therefore, a "bring it on" attitude is appropriate, rather than the patient's "white knuckling" stance. This highlights the importance of continually assessing for discrepancies in treatment goals.

Dangers of emphasizing habituation as a goal of exposure

4.5.8   Unbearable Anxiety Levels During Exposure

It is important that the patient sees high levels of anxiety (and obsessions and uncertainty) during exposure not as signs that treatment is failing, but as normal occurrences that are best used as opportunities to practice coping and enhancing distress tolerance (i.e., the "bring it on" attitude). If, however, the patient becomes extremely anxious or emotional during an exposure, and says he or she wants to stop, the exercise can be paused and the patient's concerns, discussed. You might focus this discussion on tolerance of anxiety or uncertainty in order to identify exaggerated beliefs about experiencing these feelings without ritualizing (i.e., have patients put their feelings into words). As a last resort, an alternate exposure can be substituted with the understanding that the patient will come back to the original task at a later time. If the patient is concerned that therapy isn't working because anxiety doesn't subside, it suggests the need to review the aim of exposure as fostering anxiety tolerance. If the patient is discouraged, point out that he or she took an important step simply by choosing to enter the feared situation in the first place.

4.5.9   Absence of Anxiety During Exposure

If the patient reports little or no distress during exposure, it could mean one of three things. First, the situation might no longer evoke anxiety. That is, the patient's obsessional fear has been extinguished. This is most likely to occur toward the end of treatment. In such cases, you might skip to another exposure item or conduct exposure in a different context. A second explanation is that you have not incorporated the main anxiety-evoking aspect(s) of the feared situation into the exposure task. To troubleshoot, ask the patient why the exercise does not evoke fear, or how it could be made more anxiety evoking. A third possibility is that the patient has nullified the exposure with cognitive avoidance or rituals. For example, before conducting a driving exposure, one patient called her neighbors to "warn" them to closely watch their children during the time she would be driving through the neighborhood streets. This absolved her of the responsibility for harm and therefore she did not become anxious during the driving exposure. The use of such strategies indicates a problem in understanding the treatment rationale and must be addressed in order for patients to maximally benefit from therapy.

4.5.10   Therapist Discomfort With Conducting Exposure Exercises

Despite the well-known effects of exposure-based CBT for OCD, many therapists – even those who have been trained in the delivery of exposure – either refrain from using this technique or use it sub-optimally so as to not subject patients to high levels of anxiety. Minimizing the intensity of exposure is associated with concerns about the adverse consequences of purposely confronting stimuli that will evoke high levels of discomfort (Deacon & Farrell, 2013). Recall, however, that the beneficial effects of CBT are well-documented. Reducing OCD in the long-run requires evocation of anxiety to learn how to manage this, and other OCD-related inner experiences, better. Also, exposure helps patients learn that their feared situations and thoughts pose acceptable levels of threat. Response prevention helps the patient learn that time-consuming and embarrassing rituals are not necessary to prevent feared outcomes. In fact, when the rationale for CBT is clear and the treatment plan is set up collaboratively, doing this treatment prompts a supportive and highly rewarding working relationship which helps the patient make considerable and long-lasting progress.

4.6   Multicultural Issues

OCD is observed in individuals worldwide, and culture appears to play an important role in shaping the presentation of obsessions and compulsions, which has bearing on treatment. Indeed, obsessional content stems from matters which are culturally relevant to the individual, resulting in diverse symptom expression.

In Europe, the United States, Australia, and Canada, contamination/cleaning, symmetry/ordering, taboo thoughts/mental compulsions, and doubt/checking are commonplace among OCD sufferers. In Hispanic and Latin Americans with OCD, contamination and aggression appear to be among the most common obsessions. Among Indian samples, obsessions often concern contamination and pathological doubt, with greater gender differences in symptom dimensions. In East Asian samples, contamination and symmetry are prominent, with cultural differences between Japan and China: greater need of symmetry in China and contamination and aggression in Japan. Less research is available from African cultures.

The presence of religious compulsions in OCD sufferers of different religions indicates that faith influences OCD symptoms. Among Protestant Christians, contamination and taboo (e.g., blasphemous) obsessions predominate, along with washing and mental rituals. Among Catholics, an emphasis on perfectionism has been observed; and among Jews, themes of morality and divine retribution seem to appear in obsessions. Obsessions among Islamic individuals tend to focus on purity and religious themes. OCD in Middle Eastern countries tends also reflects religious beliefs, as well as familial and societal values.

There is evidence that religious OCD symptoms respond less well to CBT than do other presentations of the problem. Specifically, it might be difficult for a patient or a clinician to distinguish between acceptable religious/moral behavior (and thoughts) versus OCD symptoms. Thus, cultural competence on the part of the therapist and a good understanding of a patient's belief system is important.

There are also important similarities in OCD presentation cross-culturally. In most cultures, for example, there are individuals with OCD who experience contamination fears along with cleaning/washing rituals. In a series of studies, a large group of investigators collected data from 777 participants in 13 countries on 6 continents (Clark & Radomsky, 2014). Although the vast majority of participants in each country experienced obsession-like intrusions, those in the United States reported the highest frequency and those in Argentina, the lowest. There were differences in the *content* of intrusions: participants from Sierra Leone reported the highest frequency of contamination-related intrusions while those from the United States and Turkey reported the highest number of religious intrusions. Cross-culturally, doubt was the most common type of intrusion. Thus, while the experience of unwanted intrusions is universal, there are differences in the content of such thoughts.

As predicted by the cognitive-behavioral model of OCD, the relationship between appraisals and thought frequency were comparable across countries; additionally, the more an intrusion was appraised as a highly unacceptable, significant, and threatening, the more it was also rated as distressing and uncontrollable. Moreover, the tendency to use reassurance seeking or a compulsive ritual to control an intrusion predicted greater frequency of distressing intrusions cross-culturally. Avoidance, distraction, thought replacement, and thought stopping, however, were relatively unrelated to the frequency or distress intrusive thoughts. These findings support the generalizability of the CBT model of obsessions cross-culturally and suggest that CBT would be the first line psychological treatment worldwide.

5

Case Vignettes

This chapter presents examples of exposure lists and treatment plans (session-by-session descriptions of situational and imaginal exposure tasks) for common presentations of OCD. CBT in each of these four cases resulted in marked improvement in quality of life as a result of successful fear extinction and reduction in compulsive rituals. You can use these vignettes as templates for building CBT programs for your own patients.

5.1   Case Vignette 1: Contamination Symptoms

Kristi, a 36-year-old hotel manager, feared contracting the herpes virus. She avoided public bathrooms and contact with surfaces such as door handles and garbage cans. She also avoided contact with other people and their belongings (pens, office telephones, etc.). Bodily waste and secretions such as urine, feces, and sweat also evoked obsessive fear. Kristi washed her hands over 50 times each day and often showered and changed her clothes multiple times to reduce her fears of contamination. If she couldn't avoid a perceived contaminant, or needed to delay washing or cleaning, Kristi would try to suppress any thoughts of herpes germs and contamination, and mentally reassure herself that she was going to be ok. Even though Kristi said that she was aware the likelihood of contracting herpes from everyday objects was very small, she remarked that she would "rather be safe than sorry" and found the anxiety she experienced in the face of contamination-related uncertainty to be overwhelming and "too strong to manage."

Kristi's exposure list was as follows (listed in order of SUDs). At each session, the specific exposure to be completed was determined randomly (an arrangement Kristi agreed to) by selecting pieces of paper out of a hat.

Item	SUDS
Door handles and hand rails	45
Images of "herpes germs"	55
Shaking hands with others	65
Public telephones	70
Images of getting cold sores from herpes	70
Garbage cans	75
Sweat	80

Item	SUDS
Images of becoming terribly ill	80
Public bathrooms	85
Urine	90
Feces	95

Kristi's response prevention plan was as follows:
- No contact with water except for one 10-min shower and two 2-min tooth brushings each day. Immediately after contact with water, she was to reexpose herself to stimuli from the fear hierarchy.
- No changing of clothes after dressing for the day.

For Kristi, sessions were structured using an expanding schedule. Specifically, sessions 1–6 were twice weekly (for 3 weeks), sessions 7–12 were once weekly (for 6 weeks), and sessions 13–16 were every other week (for 8 weeks).

During the first exposure session, Kristi practiced shaking hands with strangers (clinic staff). She also touched public telephones, concentrating on the receiver since she was concerned about germs from other peoples' mouths. Before beginning the exposure, Kristi said that she thought she could only "stand" being in contact with these objects (and tolerating the associated contamination-related thoughts and uncertainty) for 5 min. Thus, she was very surprised that she was able to manage the distress these tasks provoked for more than 20 min. Subsequent imaginal exposure involved distressing images of cold sores, uncertainty about where people might have put their hands, and who might have used the telephones she touched. Between sessions, Kristi practiced shaking hands and touching public phones, especially before eating, in a variety of different locations with varying level of difficulty (i.e., perceived dirtiness).

At the second session, Kristi and the therapist walked through the clinic and touched door handles and hand rails, maintaining contact with each for a period of several minutes. In the therapist's office, Kristi described her intrusive images of "herpes germs" crawling all over her body into an audio recorder and listened to the recording (imaginal exposure). The aim in this session was to purposely provoke feelings of anxiety and uncertainty in order for Kristi to learn that she could function even when she was feeling "dirty." Between sessions, she conducted daily self-exposures to door handles and other surfaces in a variety of places she had been avoiding, such as work and certain stores. She also practiced imaginal exposure using the recorded material. Kristi was afraid that she would have difficulty listening to the recording without the therapist present, but was surprised that she was able to do so for 20–30 min on her own.

Public bathrooms were the focus of session 3. Kristi confronted bathroom door handles, sink faucets, and soap dispensers by maintaining contact with these items for several minutes. She confronted toilets by sitting on the floor next to the bowl and touching the flusher and seat. For practice between sessions, she was instructed to sit on public toilets in various places she had been avoiding (e.g., mall bathrooms) and allow herself to "bring on" the feelings of doubt about whether these restrooms were properly cleaned. Imaginal exposure included images of germs and cold sores, as well as thoughts of uncertainty and severity of becoming ill.

During the fourth session, Kristi practiced touching garbage cans, especially those in public areas such as malls. Imaginal exposure to images of germs was continued, and Kristi practiced eating with her hands immediately after contact with trash cans. She repeated these and similar exercises each day between the fourth and fifth sessions.

Sessions 5 and 6 again involved additional supervised public bathroom exposures. At session 5, after touching the toilet, urine was confronted by having Kristi hold a paper towel dampened with a few drops of her own urine specimen collected earlier that day. Between sessions, Kristi carried the paper towel in her pocket and frequently touched it to her hands. At session 6, exposure included the introduction of feces (a piece of toilet paper lightly soiled with her own excrement). Kristi was instructed to practice with feces, urine, and toilet seats between sessions. She was surprised at her ability to perform everyday tasks (e.g., errands, work) even while feeling constantly contaminated and unsure about germs and illness.

At the seventh session, exposure to sweat was conducted by having Kristi run in place and then put one hand under her arm and the other inside her shoe. Imaginal exposure involved thinking of becoming ill from "sweat germs." Kristi kept a soiled sock in her pocket between sessions. She handled the sock each time before she ate.

Sessions 8 through 16 included repeated exposures to public bathrooms, urine, and feces. She practiced eating and touching personal items (e.g., her purse, cell phone) immediately following these exposures. Imaginal exposure to distressing thoughts and periodic contact with lesser contaminants was continued. Kristi was also encouraged to contaminate additional personal items at home and at work.

5.2   Case Vignette 2: Harming Symptoms

Steve, a 33-year-old real estate agent, performed checking rituals that were precipitated by thoughts that he could cause injury to others and their property. If he saw a fire truck or ambulance, he worried that perhaps he had started a fire or caused an accident without realizing it. He watched the news, scoured the Internet, and even checked with police to ensure he had not caused such disasters. He often returned to houses he had shown to potential buyers to make sure all appliances were off and doors locked. After his wife and children went to sleep each night, Steve spent hours checking the electrical appliances, door locks, windows, and water faucets in his own home, as well as the parking brake of his car.

Steve's exposure list was as follows:

Item	SUDS
Turn light switch on and off	45
News stories (and images) of fires	50
Open/close and lock/unlock window	55
Open/close car door and enable/disable parking break	65
News stories (and images) of accidents	70
Turn appliances on and off	75
Turn water faucet on and off	80

Steve's response prevention plan was as follows:
- No checking doors, windows, appliances, the car
- No seeking reassurance by asking other people (e.g., family, police officers) about disasters.
- No returning to other homes to check for safety.
- No watching the news or reading the local section of the newspaper to look for possible disasters.

When Steve began treatment he was in danger of losing his job because of chronic lateness caused by excessive checking. Thus, he expressed a strong desire to first confront situations and stimuli that would allow him to leave his and others' homes, and to go to bed, without checking. Accordingly, the order of exposure tasks was determined in order to prioritize helping Steve improve his quality of life and preserve his job.

The first treatment session began at Steve's home where all of the lights were first turned on. Then, Steve quickly went through the house (unsupervised by the therapist) and turned the lights off without checking (no one else was home at the time). He then left the house and drove away. For imaginal exposure back at the therapist's office, Steve practiced thinking about the possibility of a fire from accidentally leaving lights on in his haste to leave the house, and how terrible it would be to be responsible for his house burning down (and perhaps his neighbors' homes as well). Each day between the first and second sessions, as he was leaving for work (after his wife and children had already left the house for the day), Steve practiced this same exercise. Despite the amount of distress these exercises provoked, Steve was able to remain uncertain at work without returning home to check whether any fires had occurred.

The second session also began at Steve's house. Exposure involved opening and closing windows on the ground floor without checking, followed again by quickly leaving the house. Imaginal exposure involved Steve writing a script in which a burglar broke into his home and viciously murdered his wife and children when they got home from work and school (and that Steve was not there to save them). Again, between sessions, Steve practiced this exercise while his family was both home and away and at different times of day (i.e., daytime vs. nighttime), and then listed to a recording he made of himself reading the script aloud. He learned that he could experience these feelings of anxiety and doubt for much longer than he expected.

Sessions 3 and 4 also took place in Steve's home. During session 3, in addition to windows and lights, exposure included practice turning appliances on and off and then leaving the house without checking. Steve conducted imaginal exposure to images of house fires for which he was responsible because of the failure to check. At session 4, turning water faucets on and off was added to the exposure tasks. Between sessions, assignments included daily repetitions of these same exercises. Even though Steve's anxiety level was not relied on as an indicator of success, Steve found that after repeating these exposures multiple times his fear had diminished substantially from where it had been at the beginning of therapy – he was learning to be "comfortably uncomfortable" about feeling uncertain, which he found completely novel and promising.

At this point in treatment, Steve said that he was ready to apply what he had learned to his work setting. Thus, sessions 5 through 13 focused on conducting exposures at several homes for sale. Steve practiced turning lights and appliances on and off in each home, and then leaving the home and conducting imaginal exposures to thoughts of causing fires or thefts (as he had done with his own home). Between sessions, he also practiced turning lights and appliances on and off, and unlocking and locking doors and windows, before going to bed in his own home and before leaving for work. At this point in treatment, Steve was able to regain full functioning at work and was no longer in jeopardy of losing his position.

At session 14, situational exposure involved Steve and the therapist driving around the block in Steve's car, rolling down the windows, and unlocking the doors. After arriving back at the clinic, Steve turned off the car engine, applied the parking break, rolled up the windows, and locked the car doors before quickly evacuating the car and, without checking, walking into the clinic building. Imaginal exposure to thoughts about the feared consequences of leaving the parking break off, windows down, and doors unlocked, was conducted once in the therapist's office. Steve practiced similar exercises each day between sessions 14 and 15.

The focus of sessions 15 and 16 was imaginal exposure to thoughts of unknowingly causing accidents. In order to help with this task, Steve read and watched a variety of old news stories about fires and accidents and practiced imagining that he had been the one to cause the harm. Between sessions, Steve practiced these tasks and tolerating the distress, anxiety, and doubt they provoked.

5.3   Case Vignette 3: Incompleteness Symptoms

Jill, a 26-year-old woman who lived with her parents, engaged in ordering, arranging, and balancing rituals triggered by distressing obsessional thoughts of "imperfection" and "imbalance." Activities such as completing paperwork often took hours because Jill had to painstakingly make sure that letters were formed "perfectly." Items in the house had to be arranged "just so," and Jill had to ensure that such order was maintained. Her most pervasive symptoms focused on left–right balance. For example, if she used her *right* hand to open a door or to grab something (e.g., from the refrigerator), she felt an urge to repeat the behavior using her *left* hand (and vice versa) to achieve balance. These symptoms limited Jill's ability to function to the point that on many days she was unable to leave the house.

Jill's exposure list included the following items (listed here in order of SUDS). At each session, the specific exposures to be conducted were determined randomly by picking pieces of paper out of a box:

Item	SUDS
Write letters "imperfectly"	40
Write imperfectly in checkbook	55
Leave items in the family room "out of order"	67
Leave items in own bedroom "out of order"	75
Say, write, and hear the word "left" without the word "right"	75
"Notice" left–right imbalance	80
Touch items on right (or left) side only	85

Jill's response prevention plan was as follows:
- No rewriting.
- No ordering/arranging
- No "balancing rituals" (attempts to achieve left–right balance visually, verbally, behaviorally, etc.)

At session 1, Jill practiced writing letters imperfectly (e.g., sloppily); first on blank pieces of paper, then on notes she was sending to others, and finally on paperwork such as financial statements. This was also practiced between sessions. Therapy focused on Jill learning that she could tolerate the "not just right" feelings and sense of imperfection that these exposures provoked. She learned that she could experience these feelings for longer than she expected she could.

The second session involved confrontation with the word "left" in the absence of the word "right." Jill practiced saying "left" and even writing it on the back of both of her hands. Homework involved further exposure to "left." She also kept a piece of paper with this word in her pocket at all times. Again, the exposures were arranged to help Jill prove to herself that she could stick with the associated distress longer than she thought. She learned that such experiences, although uncomfortable, were manageable.

Session 3 involved continued exposure to the word "left," as well as to purposely noticing left–right imbalance and not performing any "balancing" rituals. Jill and her therapist walked through the clinic and purposely noticed unevenness (e.g., the fact that more people were sitting on the right side of the waiting room than on the left side). Jill also purposely brushed against objects such as walls and desks on her left or her right side without "balancing" this out. She completed similar exposures between sessions. In addition, she was instructed to leave her belt buckle slightly off center (slightly to the left) and to tie her left shoe noticeably more tightly than her right shoe. Jill noticed that the distress associated with these exposures was not as strong as it had been. She felt much better about evoking the unpleasant feelings.

Session 4 began with practicing writing imperfectly, this time culminating with Jill filling out her checkbook imperfectly. Homework exposure involved writing imperfectly (e.g., sloppily for other important paperwork).

At the fifth and sixth sessions, Jill practiced rearranging items in the therapist's office so that they were "not balanced." For example, she tilted the therapist's picture frames slightly to the right and shifted books on the bookshelves to the right. Jill's homework assignments involved gradually rearranging items in her own home so that they seemed "out of order." This began with items in the living room and eventually involved items in her bedroom. Jill was instructed to remind herself that these items were "out of order," but to also refrain from urges to rearrange them the "correct" way. The goal was to "bring on" the "out of order" feelings as much as possible and see that she could function in her home even with things arranged the "wrong" way. The remaining sessions involved repeated exposure to the various items confronted previously but in various different contexts. For example, after Jill created this imbalance in her bedroom, and she encouraged her parents to do the same in various parts of the house.

5.4   Case Vignette 4: Unacceptable Thoughts

Matt, was a devoutly religious 25-year-old married (heterosexual) graduate student with recurrent unwanted sexual thoughts and images involving children. These obsessions were triggered by hearing certain words (e.g., "penis") and by the sight of children – especially Matt's nephew, Todd, who was 8 years old. Matt was avoiding spending time with his family members and had stopped going to the YMCA, where he might see boys undressed in the locker room. He was also avoiding sexual intercourse with his wife because thoughts of Todd had once occurred during sex. Matt feared that the frequency and intensity of his obsessions indicated that he was becoming a pedophile. When such thoughts came to mind, he tried to "analyze" their meaning and often "tested" himself by looking at (or thinking of) adult women to reassure himself that he was still "interested" in them more than he was interested in young boys. These mental rituals sometimes lasted for hours each day. Matt also prayed ritualistically that he was not a pedophile. Matt had no history of engaging in sexual behavior with children, and he did not experience his obsessions as appetitive (i.e., fantasies).

Items on Matt's exposure list include the following (listed here in the order of SUDS):

Item	SUDS
Words ("molest" "penis" "boy" "Todd")	55
Pictures of young boys	65
Pictures of Todd	70
Spending time with Todd	75
Mental images of Todd's penis	75
YMCA locker room	75
Images of having sex with young boys	90
Sexual intercourse with wife	95

Matt's response prevention plan was as follows:
- No mental analyzing of the meaning of thoughts
- No "testing" for reassurance of attraction to adult women
- Refrain from any prayers about intrusive thoughts

Matt expressed a strong desire to be able to spend time with his family again, including with Todd. Thus, the order of exposure tasks was determined based on helping him reach this goal first.

During the first session, Matt brought pictures of Todd to look at for exposure. After a while, the therapist asked Matt to visualize what Todd would look like naked, including images of his penis. Matt was fearful that he wouldn't be able to keep these images in his mind for very long, but was surprised to find that he was able to do so for at least half an hour without praying or ritualizing. Matt was instructed to repeat this exercise each day between sessions, for longer and longer durations and in different places (e.g., home, school, mall, in a park, etc.).

At the second session, Matt again practiced viewing images of Todd again, and this time he also wrote a story describing himself having sex with Todd. Matt was instructed to vividly describe the events. He expressed concern that doing so might make him become a pedophile; thus, the exposure was engineered to help Matt embrace this uncertainty. Matt's therapist helped Matt learn that despite the distress he encountered, Matt could remain uncertain without "testing," asking for assurance, or praying. Between sessions, Matt wrote similar stories and practiced being unsure about his sexuality without performing rituals. He practiced thinking about this uncertainty in different contexts as well.

Session 3 was spent planning for an exposure in which Matt would spend an evening with Todd's family at a baseball game. Matt planned to sit next to Todd and speak with him while imagining the sexual thoughts and not ritualizing. Matt was able to complete this exposure with very few rituals, despite feeling distressed at times. Although distress level was not used as an indicator of success, Matt found that by the end of the evening, his fear had almost completely subsided – Matt felt comfortable being near Todd and having sexual thoughts and uncertainty. At the following session, the therapist reminded Matt that there was still no guarantee that Matt was not a pedophile – and yet he was able to feel comfortable. Matt was surprised at this achievement.

During the fourth exposure session, Matt practiced saying the words "molest," "penis," "boy," "anal sex," and "blow job," which provoked anxiety for him. He also repeatedly wrote these words on sheets of paper that he kept in his wallet. Homework practice included repeating these exercises daily and discovering that the distress associated with these words was manageable.

At session 5, Matt viewed pictures of young male fashion models on the Internet. He was instructed to discuss how attractive he thought these boys were. He repeated this task between sessions with an emphasis on remaining uncertain regarding whether he was attracted to these boys more than he was attracted to his wife. Matt found that this uncertainty was more bearable than he had predicted it would be.

During sessions 6 to 10, Matt practiced viewing more pictures of boys (fashion models) in swim suits and writing stories about having sexual encounters with them. These "fantasies" were varied according to what evoked greater distress; for example, the use of more graphic imagery. Matt also was instructed to resume intercourse with his wife and to resist urges to dismiss any intrusive thoughts about boys that came to mind. Matt used these exposures to further disconfirm his beliefs about the intolerability of uncertainty about his sexual orientation.

Exposure to locker rooms at the YMCA and other area swimming clubs occurred following the 11th session (which was used to plan these exposures). By this time, Matt felt comfortable performing exposures on his own. Matt planned to enter the boy's/men's locker room, let his eyes wander and imagine sexual encounters. He also allowed himself to remain uncertain about his "true" sexuality and refrained from prayer rituals and analyzing his thoughts.

6

Further Reading

Abramowitz, J. (2006). *Understanding and treating obsessive-compulsive disorder: A cognitive-behavioral approach.* New York, NY: Lawrence Erlbaum Associates.
Presents didactic material on the clinical features and psychological theories of OCD. Also contains a manual for cognitive-behavioral assessment and treatment.

Abramowitz, J., Franklin, M., & Cahill, S. (2003). Approaches to common obstacles in the exposure-based treatment of obsessive-compulsive disorder. *Cognitive and Behavioral Practice, 10,* 14–22. http://doi.org/10.1016/S1077-7229(03)80004-4
This article discusses a number of problems that can arise during CBT for OCD. Case examples are presented and suggestions for managing these problems are described.

Abramowitz, J. S., & Arch, J. J. (2014). Strategies for improving long-term outcomes in cognitive behavioral therapy for obsessive-compulsive disorder: Insights from learning theory. *Cognitive and Behavioral Practice, 21,* 20–31. doi:10.1016/j.cbpra.2013.06.004 http://doi.org/10.1016/j.cbpra.2013.06.004
This article discusses methods for optimizing long-term treatment outcome following ERP for OCD based on principles of learning and memory.

Craske, M. G., Treanor, M., Conway, C. C., Zbozinek, T., & Vervliet, B. (2014). Maximizing exposure therapy: An inhibitory learning approach. *Behaviour Research and Therapy, 58,* 10–23. doi:10.1016/j.brat.2014.04.006 http://doi.org/10.1016/j.brat.2014.04.006
This article provides clinical examples, including case vignettes, of how clinicians can apply the inhibitory learning model to exposure therapy for anxiety disorders.

7

References

Abramovitch, A., Abramowitz, J. S., & Mittleman, A. (2013). The neuropsychology of adult obsessive-compulsive disorder: A meta-analysis. *Clinical Psychology Review, 33*, 1163–1171. http://doi.org/10.1016/j.cpr.2013.09.004

Abramowitz, J. S., Baucom, D. H., Wheaton, M. G., Boeding, S., Fabricant, L. E., Paprocki, C., & Fischer, M. S. (2013). Enhancing exposure and response prevention for OCD: A couple-based approach. *Behavior Modification, 37*, 189–210. http://doi.org/10.1177/0145445512444596

Abramowitz, J. S., Deacon, B., Olatunji, B., Wheaton, M. G., Berman, N., Losardo, D., . . . Hale, L. (2010). Assessment of obsessive-compulsive symptom dimensions: Development and evaluation of the Dimensional Obsessive-Compulsive Scale. *Psychological Assessment, 22*, 180–198. http://doi.org/10.1037/a0018260

American Psychiatric Association. (2013). *Diagnostic and Statistical Manual of Mental Disorders (5th ed.)*. Arlington, VA: Author.

Clark, D. A., & Radomsky, A. (2014). Introduction: A global perspective on unwanted thoughts. *Journal of Obsessive-Compulsive and Related Disorders, 3*(3), 265–268. http://doi.org/10.1016/j.jocrd.2014.02.001

Craske, M., & Barlow, D. H. (2006). *Mastery of your anxiety and panic (therapist guide)*. New York, NY: Oxford University Press.

Craske, M., Treanor, M., Conway, C., Zbozinek, T., & Vervliet, B. (2014). Maximizing exposure therapy: An inhibitory learning approach. *Behaviour Research and Therapy, 58*, 10–23. http://doi.org/10.1016/j.brat.2014.04.006

Crino, R. D., & Andrews, G. (1996a). Obsessive-compulsive disorder and Axis I comorbidity. *Journal of Anxiety Disorders, 10*(1), 37–46. http://doi.org/10.1016/0887-6185(95)00033-X

Crino, R. D., & Andrews, G. (1996b). Personality disorder in obsessive compulsive disorder: A controlled study. *Journal of Psychiatric Research, 30*(1), 29–38. http://doi.org/10.1016/0022-3956(95)00043-7

Deacon, B. J., & Farrell, N. R. (2013). Therapist barriers in the dissemination of exposure therapy. In E. Storch & D. McKay (Eds.), *Treating variants and complications in anxiety disorders* (pp. 363–373). New York, NY: Springer.

Di Nardo, P., Brown, T., & Barlow, D. H. (1994). *Anxiety Disorders Interview Schedule for DSM-IV: Lifetime Version (ADIS-IV-LV)*. San Antonio, TX: The Psychological Corporation.

Eisen, J. L., Phillips, K. A., Baer, L., Beer, D. A., Atala, K. D., & Rasmussen, S. A. (1998). The Brown Assessment of Beliefs Scale: Reliability and validity. *American Journal of Psychiatry, 155*(1), 102–108.

First, M. B., Spitzer, R. L., Gibbon, M., & Williams, J. (2002). *Structured Clinical Interview for the DSM-IV Axis 1 Disorders*. New York, NY: Biometrics Research Department, New York State Psychiatric Institute.

Foa, E. B., Huppert, J. D., & Cahill, S. P. (2006). Emotional processing theory: An update. In B. O. Rothbaum (Ed.), *Pathological anxiety: Emotional processing in etiology and treatment* (pp. 3–24). New York, NY: Guilford Press.

Foa, E., & Kozak, M. (1986). Emotional processing of fear: Exposure to corrective information. *Psychological Bulletin, 99*, 20–35. http://doi.org/10.1037/0033-2909.99.1.20

Foa, E., Liebowitz, M. R., Kozak, M. J., Davies, S., Campeas, R., Franklin, M. E., ... Tu, X. (2005). Randomized, placebo-controlled trial of exposure and ritual prevention, clomipramine, and their combination in the treatment of obsessive-compulsive disorder. *American Journal of Psychiatry, 162*, 151–161. http://doi.org/10.1176/appi.ajp.162.1.151

Franklin, M. E., Abramowitz, J. S., Foa, E. B., Kozak, M. J., & Levitt, J. T. (2000). Effectiveness of exposure and ritual prevention for obsessive-compulsive disorder: Randomized compared with nonrandomized samples. *Journal of Consulting and Clinical Psychology, 68*(4), 594–602. http://doi.org/10.1037/0022-006X.68.4.594

Frost, R. O., & Steketee, S. (2002). *Cognitive approaches to obsessions and compulsions: Theory, assessment, and treatment.* Oxford, UK: Elsevier.

Goodman, W. K., Price, L. H., Rasmussen, S. A., Mazure, C., Delgado, P., Heninger, G. R., … Charney, D. S. (1989). The Yale-Brown Obsessive Compulsive Scale: Validity. *Archives of General Psychiatry, 46*, 1012–1016. http://doi.org/10.1001/archpsyc.1989.01810110048007

Goodman, W. K., Price, L. H., Rasmussen, S. A., Mazure, C., Fleischmann, R. L., Hill, C. L., Heninger, G. R., & Charney, D. S. (1989). The Yale-Brown Obsessive Compulsive Scale: Development, use, and reliability. *Archives of General Psychiatry, 46*, 1006–1011. http://doi.org/10.1001/archpsyc.1989.01810110048007

Hayes, S. C., Strosahl, K. D., & Wilson, K. G. (2011). *Acceptance and commitment therapy: The process and practice of mindful change* (2nd ed.). New York, NY: Guilford Press.

Kozak, M. J., & Coles, M. E. (2005). Treatment of obsessive-compulsive disorder: Unleashing the power of exposure. In J. S. Abramowitz & A. C. Houts (Eds.), *Concepts and controversies in obsessive-compulsive disorder* (pp. 283–304). New York, NY: Springer.

McKay, D., Abramowitz, J. S., Calamari, J. E., Kyrios, M., Radomsky, A. S., Sookman, D., Taylor, S. & Wilhelm, S. (2004). A critical evaluation of obsessive-compulsive disorder subtypes: Symptoms versus mechanisms. *Clinical Psychology Review, 24*, 283–313. http://doi.org/10.1016/j.cpr.2004.04.003

Mowrer, O. (1960). *Learning theory and behavior.* New York, NY: Wiley. http://doi.org/10.1037/10802-000

Obsessive Compulsive Cognitions Working Group. (2005). Psychometric validation of the Obsessive Belief Questionnaire and Interpretation of Intrusions Inventory – Part 2: Factor analyses and testing of a brief version. *Behaviour Research and Therapy, 43*(11), 1527–1542. http://doi.org/10.1016/j.brat.2004.07.010

Olatunji, B., Davis, M., Powers, M., & Smits, J. (2013). Cognitive-behavioral therapy for obsessive-compulsive disorder: A meta-analysis of treatment outcome and moderators. *Journal of Psychiatric Research, 47*, 33–41. http://doi.org/10.1016/j.jpsychires.2012.08.020

Rachman, S., & Hodgson, R. (1980). *Obsessions and compulsions.* Englewood Cliffs, NJ: Prentice Hall.

Ruscio, A., Stein, D. J., Chiu, D., & Kessler, R. (2010). The epidemiology of obsessive-compulsive disorder in the national comorbidity survey replication. *Molecular Psychiatry, 15*, 53–63. http://doi.org/10.1038/mp.2008.94

Sheehan, D. (1983). *The anxiety disease.* New York, NY: Charles Scribner and Sons.

Twohig, M. G., Hayes, S. G., Plumb, J. C., Pruitt, L. D., Collins, A. B., Hazlett-Stevens, H., & Woldneck, M. R. (2010). A randomized clinical trial of acceptance and commitment therapy versus progressive relaxation training for obsessive-compulsive disorder. *Journal of Consulting and Clinical Psychology, 78*, 705–716. http://doi.org/10.1037/a0020508

Williams, K., Chambless, D. L., & Steketee, G. (1998). Behavioral treatment of obsessive-compulsive disorder in African Americans: Clinical issues. *Journal of Behavior Therapy and Experimental Psychiatry, 29*(2), 163–170. http://doi.org/10.1016/S0005-7916(98)00004-4

8

Appendix: Tools and Resources

Functional Assessment of OCD Symptoms

Date: _____

Patient Name: _____   Present age: _____

Date of birth: _____   Duration of symptoms: _____

Educational level: _____

Obsessional Stimuli

- **External triggers of obsessions** (people, places, things, and situations that evoke anxiety; e.g., mold, leaving home, "13")

_____

_____

_____   ___

_____

_____

_____

_____

- **Obsessional thoughts, impulses, images, doubts** (e.g., "God is dead," images of germs, impulse to harm, doubts about fires)

_____

_____

_____

_____

_____

_____

_____

Cognitive Features

- **Feared consequences of exposure to obsessional triggers** (e.g., "I will get sick if I don't wash my hands")

_____

_____

_____

_____

_____

_____

_____

- **Catastrophic interpretations of intrusive thoughts** (e.g., "thinking about it is the same as doing it")

_____

_____

_____

_____

_____

_____

_____

- **Fears of long-term anxiety/discomfort** ("I will be anxious forever unless I ritualize")

_____

_____

_____

_____

_____

_____

Responses to Obsessional Distress (Safety-Seeking Behaviors)

- **Passive avoidance** (identify its relationship to obsessional fear; e.g., avoids old buildings due to fears of asbestos)

_____

_____

_____

_____

_____

_____

- **Overt compulsive rituals** (identify relationships to obsessional fear; e.g., checks the door to prevent burglary; reassurance seeking)

_____

_____

_____

_____

_____

_____

_____

- **Mental rituals, covert neutralizing strategies** (e.g., thought suppression, mental reviewing, using positive images; identify relationships to obsessional fear)

_____

_____

_____

_____

_____

_____

_____

_____

Self-Monitoring of OCD Symptoms

Ritual 1: _____ Ritual 1: _____

Date	Time	What triggered the ritual? (brief summary of situation or thought)	Time spent with ritual	
			1	2

Everyone Has Intrusive Thoughts

In obsessive-compulsive disorder (OCD), *obsessions* are defined as unwanted intrusive thoughts, ideas, or images that trigger anxiety, fear, uncertainty, and discomfort. The content of obsessions is often senseless or bizarre. The themes of obsessions often concern harm, violence, aggression, sex, religion, mistakes, physical appearance, germs, diseases, need for exactness, among other things. Because obsessions evoke anxiety and distress, people usually try to resist, stop, control, or get reassurance about these intrusive thoughts. But this often doesn't work, or perhaps it works only for a short time. Then, the thought returns and can develop a "life of its own."

What many people do not realize is that practically everyone experiences unwanted intrusive thoughts (whether or not they have OCD). These sorts of thoughts are as much a part of normal human thinking as are fantasies and daydreams about positive events. The focus of this handout is to teach you that the unpleasant, distressing, repugnant, bizarre, and senseless obsessional thoughts that you are experiencing are not dangerous or abnormal.

Intrusive Thoughts Are Normal

Everyone knows the experience of senseless intrusive thoughts and doubts. Whether it is a daydream about winning the lottery, a frightening image of harm or danger, or a senseless doubt that is completely opposite of how you usually think, all humans have nonsensical and unwanted thoughts and doubts. You may be surprised to learn that pretty much everyone in the world has the kinds of intrusive, upsetting, and inappropriate unwanted thoughts that resemble obsessions in OCD. That is, *people without OCD experience the same kinds of unwanted and intrusive thoughts as do people with OCD.* The list below shows some examples of intrusive thoughts reported by people *without* OCD:

- Thought of jumping off the bridge onto the highway below
- Thought of running my car off the road or onto oncoming traffic
- Thought of poking something into my eyes
- Impulse to jump onto the tracks as the train comes into the station
- Image of hurting or killing a loved one
- Idea of doing something mean towards an elderly person or a small baby
- Thought of wishing that a person would die
- Impulse to run over a pedestrian who walks too slowly
- Impulse to slap someone who talks too much
- Thought of something going terribly wrong because of my error
- Thought of accidentally hitting someone with my car
- Image of a loved one being injured or killed
- Thought of receiving news of a close relative's death
- Idea that other people might think that I am guilty of stealing
- Thought of being poked in the eye by an umbrella
- Thought of being trapped in a car under water
- Thought of catching diseases from various places such as a toilet
- Thought of dirt that is always on my hand
- Thought of contracting a disease from contact with another person
- Urge to insult a friend for no apparent reason
- Image of screaming at my relatives
- Impulse to say something nasty or inappropriate to someone
- Impulse to do something shameful or terrible
- Thought that I left a door unlocked

- Thought of my house getting broken into while I'm not home
- Thought that I left an appliance on and cause a fire
- Thought of sexually molesting young children
- Thought that my house burned down and I lost everything I own
- Thought that is contrary to my moral and religious beliefs
- Hoping someone doesn't succeed
- Thoughts of smashing a table full of crafts made of glass
- Thoughts of acts of violence during sex
- Sexual impulses that are contrary to my sexual orientation
- Thought of "unnatural" sexual acts
- Image of a penis
- Image of grandparents having sex
- Thought about objects not arranged perfectly

Why do all people get these kinds of intrusive thoughts? This is probably because as humans we have highly developed and creative brains that can imagine all kinds of scenarios – some more pleasant than others. Sometimes, our "thought generator" produces thoughts about danger even though there may not be any real threat present. Humans have many thoughts while awake and during sleep, so it would be expected that our brains would sometimes create bizarre or senseless thoughts ("mental noise"). Often, such thoughts are triggered by actual situations such driving, seeing a weapon, using the bathroom, hearing words associated with sex, or seeing a religious icon.

Scientists have conducted many studies on unwanted intrusive thoughts in people with and without OCD. All of these studies confirm that people with and without OCD have the same kinds of intrusive thoughts. In the most well-known study, researchers asked people with OCD and people without OCD to list some of their unpleasant unwanted thoughts. The lists (which resembled the list of thoughts shown above) were then given to psychologists and psychiatrists who were asked to say which thoughts came from people with and without OCD. But most of the time, even these professionals could not tell from whom the thoughts came.

This study (and several others like it) confirms that people with OCD do not have something wrong with their brains or minds that causes them to have the kinds of obsessive thoughts they have. That is, people with OCD are not mad, bad, or dangerous. Instead, obsessions in OCD (even the most unacceptable, disgusting, violent, depraved thoughts and images) develop from entirely normal obsessional experiences, as we will explore in this handout.

Differences Between "Normal" and "OCD" Obsessions

Researchers *have* found some important differences between "normal" obsessions and clinical (OCD) obsessions. In particular:
1. OCD obsessions are *more distressing* than normal obsessions,
2. OCD obsessions are *resisted more strongly* than are normal obsessions, and
3. OCD obsessions are *more repetitive* than normal obsessions.

The rest of this handout will explain these differences so that you understand how distressing (anxiety-provoking), recurring, and intense OCD obsessions develop from normal everyday intrusive thoughts (normal obsessions).

From: J. S. Abramowitz and R. J. Jacoby: *Obsessive-Compulsive Disorder in Adults*   © 2015 Hogrefe Publishing

A. Why Are OCD Obsessions Distressing?

Although everyone has unwanted distressing intrusive thoughts, it turns out that people have different ways of relating to, or interpreting the meaning of, these kinds of thoughts. When such thoughts are interpreted as especially threatening, it causes the thoughts to evoke fear, anxiety, and distress.

Let's look at how people with and without OCD relate to and interpret their intrusive unwanted thoughts. First, research shows that people *without* OCD regard their intrusive unwanted thoughts as "mental noise." In other words, they recognize that such thoughts (even thoughts about disturbing topics) are probably meaningless. For example, a person without OCD who experiences an unwanted thought might say to him or herself, "that's a silly thought," or "that doesn't make sense." When this happens, the person merely observes that the thought is present, but doesn't resist or try to control the thought. As a result, the thought might pass out of consciousness, or it might hang around for a while but the person is indifferent.

On the other hand, people with OCD tend to *misinterpret* these normal intrusive thoughts as very meaningful, significant, threatening or dangerous, and needing to be controlled. For example:

- "It is bad to have this kind of thought"
- "If I am thinking of something bad, it must be true"
- "If I think of something awful, it means I am an awful person"
- "If I have bad thoughts, it means I am losing my mind or that I will do something terrible"
- "I need to get rid of these kinds of thoughts"

When a person interprets his or her own thoughts as dangerous or threatening, this is what makes him or her feel distressed and anxious. After all, if you truly believe that having an unwanted thought means that something bad is about to happen, or that you are a bad person, it's normal to feel afraid and unsure. However, it is important to see that the real problem is the mistaken interpretation of the intrusive thought, not the thought itself. The thought is a normal experience. *Misinterpreting normal intrusive thoughts as significant or dangerous makes the thoughts become distressing.*

B. Why Are OCD Obsessions Resisted?

Misinterpreting certain unwanted intrusive thoughts as dangerous leads not only to distress, but it also makes you want to resist or push the thought out of your mind. You can probably see how someone would try to resist an intrusive upsetting negative thought if they interpreted this thought to be significant, important, or dangerous.

C. Why Are OCD Obsessions Repetitive?

People with OCD report that their obsessional thoughts are repetitive (they occur more frequently than do normal obsessions). Sometimes such thoughts are triggered by reminders in the environment, but at other times, they just seem to pop up "out of the blue." The repetitiousness of obsessions also has a lot to do with how a person relates to and interprets these kinds of thoughts.

Specifically, once an intrusive thought is interpreted as threatening, it activates the body's automatic danger detection system (the "fight-flight" system) which causes the person to become hyper alert and "on guard" for the perceived threat. This is a helpful response whenever real threat is present because it helps protect us from danger. For instance, if you had to walk across a busy street, your "fight or flight" response would kick in and you would become very aware of the cars coming toward you. You would scan the road for cars so that you could run out of the way to safety (*flight*) if you had to.

In the case of OCD obsessions, however, the perceived threat is just a thought that has been *misinterpreted* as threatening. So, this leads to becoming hyper-aware of (preoccupied with) unwanted thought as if they were truly dangerous (which, as we have seen, is not the case). Having this kind of relationship with intrusive thoughts helps explain why such thoughts become repetitive.

From: J. S. Abramowitz and R. J. Jacoby: *Obsessive-Compulsive Disorder in Adults*   © 2015 Hogrefe Publishing

There are other ways that people with OCD respond to intrusive thoughts that can increase the repetitiveness of obsessions. For example, humans are not very good at controlling their thoughts. So, trying to push unwanted thoughts out of your head (called *thought suppression*) actually leads to an *increase* in the unwanted thought. This is a normal phenomenon – just see what happens if you try *not* to think of a pink elephant. If you have intrusive thoughts that you have misinterpreted as dangerous, leading you to try to force the thoughts out of your mind, you will probably end up with more of the unwanted thought (leading to a vicious cycle of more anxiety and futile attempts to suppress, and so on).

A useful metaphor for thinking about this idea is *"if you don't want it, you'll have it."* This applies to obsessions in that trying to control, resist, or dismiss obsessional thoughts (and the experiences of doubt and anxiety) only leads to becoming more preoccupied with them (because obsessions become something to obsess about).

Conclusions

In conclusion, it is important to realize that everyone has intrusive, unwanted, upsetting thoughts from time to time. These thoughts, and the experiences of anxiety and doubt that accompany them, are normal. They do not suggest any danger, evil, ungodliness, perversion, immorality, etc. They are simply senseless thoughts. The major difference between people with and without OCD is in how one relates to these kinds of thoughts, and how they are interpreted. People with OCD relate to their obsessional thoughts as if these thoughts were significant, meaningful, dangerous, and needing to be controlled. This leads to anxiety and distress. It also makes the thoughts seem to take on a "life of their own." One aim of treatment for OCD is to help you learn how to properly regard these thoughts as "mental noise" so that when they show up – as they do for everyone – they don't have to cause you problems.

From: J. S. Abramowitz and R. J. Jacoby: *Obsessive-Compulsive Disorder in Adults*   © 2015 Hogrefe Publishing

Exposure List

Items	SUDS
1.	
2.	
3.	
4.	
5.	
6.	
7.	
8.	
9.	
10.	
11.	
12.	
13.	
14.	
15.	
16.	
17.	
18.	
19.	
20.	

From: J. S. Abramowitz and R. J. Jacoby: *Obsessive-Compulsive Disorder in Adults* © 2015 Hogrefe Publishing

Guidelines for Conducting Exposure

1. **Exposure practices should be structured.** Prepare for the exercise in advance (as needed) to make sure that it is conducted properly and that you have any materials you might need. Decide what you will do in the situation and how long you will stay. Plan when you will complete your practice and put it in your schedule. Have a back-up plan in case the original does not work out.

2. **Exposure practices should be repeated frequently and in different contexts.** Practice the same exposure tasks over and over and under different conditions to maximize learning.

3. **Vary up your exposure practices.** Push yourself to practice exposures in a random order – not simply starting with the easiest situations and going gradually. Decide on exposure tasks based on your life values or pick them at random. Challenge yourself!

4. **Expect to feel uncomfortable.** Exposure tasks typically evoke discomfort. This discomfort, however, is necessary for you to learn how to handle obsessions in a healthier way. And whether or not it subsides as you remain in the exposure, you will learn something important. Success should not be judged by how you felt in the situation. Rather, success should be judged by whether you were able to stay in the situation *despite* feeling anxious.

5. **Try not to fight your fear.** Anxiety and fear are the raw materials of change. You will not benefit from exposure if you fight them. Instead of trying to make anxiety, uncertainty, and distress *go away*, you are learning to be *better* at having these feelings.

6. **Don't use subtle avoidance strategies.** Complete exposure practices without using distraction, anti-anxiety medication, alcohol, and other such anxiety-reduction strategies.

7. **Use exposure practices to test negative predictions about the consequences of facing your fear.** Before starting the exposure, think about what you are afraid might happen during the task and how long you can stick with it. Then conduct the exposure practice to test the accuracy of your fearful prediction. Afterwards, review what you learned from the exposure and how it compares to what you expected. Did the worst possible thing happen? How did you manage?

8. **Keep track of your fear level.** Pay attention to how you are feeling during the exposure task. Take note of your anxiety level at regular intervals and rate your fear level from 0–100. This will teach you that you can manage different levels of anxiety.

9. **Exposure should last until you have tested a prediction.** Continue the exposure until you have demonstrated that what you feared is unlikely to happen, or that you can handle feelings of anxiety and uncertainty about your obsessions. Try to surprise yourself with what you learn from exposures.

10. **Practice exercises by yourself.** It is helpful to conduct some exposures by yourself because the presence of other people can sometimes make us feel artificially safe.

From: J. S. Abramowitz and R. J. Jacoby: *Obsessive-Compulsive Disorder in Adults* © 2015 Hogrefe Publishing

Exposure Practice Form

Date: Time: Place: ____ Alone ____Accompanied (*check one*)

Before You Start

1. Describe the exposure (*What fears will you face and what anxiety-reduction strategies will you give up?*)

2. What do you most fear will happen when you try this exposure? (*be specific*)

3. How long do you think you can stick with this task? _____

During the Exposure

1. Every _____ minutes during the exposure note (a) your anxiety level and (b) the strength of your urge to do anxiety-reducing behaviors on a 0–100 scale.

Anxiety	Urge	Anxiety	Urge	Anxiety	Urge	Anxiety	Urge
1. ____	____	6. ____	____	11. ____	____	16. ____	____
2. ____	____	7. ____	____	12. ____	____	17. ____	____
3. ____	____	8. ____	____	13. ____	____	18. ____	____
4. ____	____	9. ____	____	14. ____	____	19. ____	____
5. ____	____	10. ____	____	15. ____	____	20. ____	____

2. Describe your feelings during the exposure. (*use phrases like "I'm feeling very scared about…"*)

After the Exposure

1. Describe the outcome of the exposure in relation to your answers to questions #2 and #3 (*What happened? Did your fears come true? How did your feelings of fear and anxiety respond? How did you get through the experience? What would happen if you tried it again?*):

2. What did you learn from this experience? In what ways were you surprised by what happened?

3. What could you do to vary up this exposure?

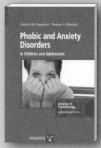

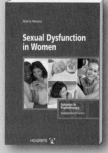
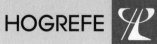

View all volumes at www.hogrefe.com/series/apt

Hogrefe Publishing
30 Amberwood Parkway · Ashland, OH 44805 · USA
Tel: (800) 228-3749 · Fax: (419) 281-6883
E-Mail: customerservice@hogrefe.com

Hogrefe Publishing
Merkelstr. 3 · 37085 Göttingen · Germany
Tel: +49 551 999 500 · Fax: +49 551 999 50 111
E-Mail: customerservice@hogrefe.de

Hogrefe Publishing c/o Marston Book Services Ltd
160 Eastern Ave., Milton Park· Abingdon, OX14 4SB · UK
Tel: +44 1235 465577 · Fax +44 1235 465556
direct.orders@marston.co.uk

HOGREFE

Order online at **www.hogrefe.com**
or call toll-free **(800) 228-3749** (US only)

Jonathan S. Abramowitz & Autumn E. Braddock

Hypochondriasis and Health Anxiety

In the series: *Advances in Psychotherapy – Evidence-Based Practice* - Vol. 19

2010, x + 94 pages, ISBN 978-0-88937-325-9
US $29.80 / £ 19.90 / € 24.95
(Series Standing Order: US $24.80 / £ 15.90 / € 19.95)

An essential resource for anyone providing services for individuals with somatoform or anxiety disorders

Cognitive-behavioral therapy is now the treatment of choice for individuals with health anxiety and related problems. The latest research shows that it results in reductions in health-related worries, reassurance-seeking behavior, and phobic avoidance, as well as increases in life satisfaction and everyday functioning.

This compact, easy to understand book by experts Jonathan S. Abramowitz and Autumn E. Braddock opens with an overview of the diagnostic issues and assessment of health anxiety, and delineates a research-based conceptual framework for understanding the development, maintenance, and treatment of this problem.

The focus of the book is a highly practical guide to implementing treatment, packed with helpful clinical pearls, therapist-patient dialogues, illustrative case vignettes, and sample forms and handouts. Readers are equipped with skills for engaging reluctant patients in treatment and tailoring educational, cognitive, and behavioral techniques for health-related anxiety. The book, which also addresses common obstacles in treatment, represents an essential resource for anyone providing services for individuals with somatoform or anxiety disorders.

Jonathan S. Abramowitz · Autumn E. Braddock

Hypochondriasis and Health Anxiety

Advances in Psychotherapy
Evidence-Based Practice

HOGREFE

**For further details visit
www.hogrefe.com**

About the Authors:

Jonathan S. Abramowitz, Ph.D, ABPP, is Professor and Associate Chair of Psychology at the University of North Carolina at Chapel Hill. He is an international expert on the treatment of anxiety disorders, having published over 150 research articles, book chapters, and books. He regularly presents workshops for clinicians on the treatment of anxiety disorders.

Autumn E. Braddock, PhD, is a primary care psychologist within the Veterans Affairs Greater Los Angeles Healthcare System, specializing in behavioral medicine and cognitive-behavioral therapy for anxiety disorders. She has presented her research, primarily addressing anxiety within medical populations, at national and international conferences.

Hogrefe Publishing
30 Amberwood Parkway · Ashland, OH 44805 · USA
Tel: (800) 228-3749 · Fax: (419) 281-6883
E-Mail: customerservice@hogrefe.com

Hogrefe Publishing
Merkelstr. 3 · 37085 Göttingen · Germany
Tel: +49 551 999 500 · Fax: +49 551 999 50 425
E-Mail: customerservice@hogrefe.de

Hogrefe Publishing c/o Marston Book Services Ltd
160 Eastern Ave., Milton Park · Abingdon, OX14 4SB · UK
Tel: +44 1235 465577 · Fax +44 1235 465556
E-mail: direct.orders@marston.co.uk

 HOGREFE

**Order online at www.hogrefe.com
or call toll-free (800) 228-3749 (US only)**